Defiant Children

Defiant Children
A Clinician's Manual
for Parent Training

RUSSELL A. BARKLEY
University of Massachusetts Medical Center

THE GUILFORD PRESS
New York   *London*

To my parents
Mildred M. Barkley
Donald S. Barkley

©1987 The Guilford Press
A Division of Guilford Publications, Inc.
72 Spring Street, New York, N.Y. 10012

Printed in the United States of America

Last digit is print number: 9 8 7 6 5 4 3 2 1

Library of Congress Cataloging in Publication Data

Barkley, Russell A., 1949–
    Defiant children.

    Bibliography: p.
    Includes index.
    1. Parenting—Study and teaching. 2. Behavior modification—Study and teaching. I. Title.
HQ755.7.B37   1987   649'.1'07   86-25796
ISBN 0-89862-700-1

Preface

This manual is an effort to set forth a sequence of procedures for training parents in child management skills that I have used with a variety of behavior disordered children during the past 10 years of my clinical practice and that, in large measure, are the culmination of over 20 years of research and clinical experience by others. For the past 5 years, I have taught these procedures to over 3,000 mental health professionals in more than 30 major cities in the United States and Canada as part of a series of 1-day workshops. The response to these workshops has been most gratifying. The majority of those attending not only found these procedures to be extremely useful in their clinical practice with families, but also encouraged me to develop a manual of the techniques that could serve as a clinical handbook, allowing wider dissemination to child mental health workers. I am genuinely grateful to those individuals for this encouragement.

The roots of this parent training program begin in a set of methods developed more than 20 years ago by Constance Hanf, professor emeritus at the University of Oregon Health Sciences Center. The program, referred to as a "two-stage program" for child noncompliance, consisted at that time of two fundamental procedures designed to teach parents more effective ways of dealing with child noncompliance. Parents were first taught an effective method of attending positively to ongoing appropriate child behaviors, particularly compliance with requests, while ignoring inappropriate behavior. After this, parents were instructed in a second procedure consisting of the immediate use of time out from reinforcement, contingent upon child noncompliance with a command. In combination, these procedures proved a powerful treatment package for families dealing with noncompliance in their children. Practice of the methods in the clinic under therapist supervision was an essential part of this program as was the use of simply worded, brief handouts on the use of the methods at home. Many psychology interns and fellows, including the author, were blessed with the opportunity to acquire these skills during our training at the Health Sciences Center with Dr. Hanf, as the procedures had not been published or widely disseminated. Those wishing to read more extensively about the original program can now refer to the text by Forehand and McMahon (1981) for the details of the procedures as well as the extensive research Dr. Forehand and his colleagues and students have conducted over the past 10 years.

During the past 10 years of using this program, I have had occasion to expand and modify it to deal with populations of hyperactive, attention deficit disordered, conduct disordered, or more seriously behaviorally disturbed children. An introductory session has been added to explain more fully to parents the development of misbehavior, and especially noncompliance, in their children. More details are also provided on teaching parents not only to reinforce direct compliance with requests but also to encourage children to play independently of their parents when the parents cannot be interrupted. The inclusion of a variation of the Home Chip Program (Christophersen, Barnard, & Barnard, 1981) in a modified form was necessitated by the realization that seriously and chronically behavior disordered children are not as consistently responsive to social praise and affection as are normal children. Hence, a more powerful means of reinforcing child behavior was needed to increase and sustain child compliance with parental requests. Sessions have also been added to address specific problems in dealing with noncompliant child behavior in public places, to train children in a "think aloud–think ahead" self-control technique, and to prepare parents to manage future misbehavior that may arise from the child. Despite these changes, I have tried to remain true to the principles of the original program: the requirements of clinic and in-home practice of the methods by the parents, and the use of brief, simply worded parent handouts.

The program described here owes much to the stimulating, heuristic, and collaborative discussions I have had over the years with others trained in the original program. Charles Cunningham, Eric Mash, and Eric Ward have been the most instrumental in my modification of the program and formulation of new program components based upon current research and clinical practice. The writings of and my discussions with Rex Forehand and Robert McMahon, and the faculty at the Child Development and Rehabilitation Center, University of Oregon Health Sciences Center, have also made significant contributions to this program.

I am indebted to Peter Wengert, editor at The Guilford Press, for his encouragement of this project and his tolerance of the many delays in my completing it because of the demands of an extensive clinical, research, and teaching practice. I continue to express my sincere gratitude to my wife and children, who unselfishly gave of their family time so that this project might be completed. The wisdom I have gained from the unique experiences with my own children is undoubtedly woven into the fabric of ideas expressed here. Finally, I owe a great deal to the more than 800 families of behavior problem children to whom I have had the fortunate experience to personally teach this program. Many of their suggestions for improving the program are contained herein.

Russell A. Barkley, Ph.D.
Worcester, Massachusetts

Contents

Introduction

PURPOSES OF PROGRAM

This manual is designed to serve several purposes. First, it sets forth detailed instructions on conducting a highly effective, empirically validated program for the clinical training of parents in the management of behavior problem children. Second, it provides a series of parent handouts to be used during the course of the program. These handouts include various rating scales and forms to be completed by the parent, as well as instructions to the parent for use with each step of the program. The handouts are designed to be easy to read and brief. They are not meant to be used without training by a skilled child/family therapist. Finally, the manual outlines methods of assessment that the trainer may wish to employ in the initial evaluation of the child and family or in the periodic evaluation of treatment effects throughout training.

It must be made clear at the beginning that this manual and the program it describes are intended for use by individuals who have had education and training in the knowledge and skills necessary to provide psychological services to children and their families. Professionals using this program should have adequate training in child development, child psychopathology, social learning and behavior modification techniques, and other clinical interventions with families. In short, this program is not a substitute for general clinical training nor the careful exercise of clinical judgment and ethics in dealing with behavior problem children and their families. The utmost care is always required in tailoring these methods to the characteristics of a particular child and his or her family.

This manual is not intended to be a review of the scientific literature on parent training programs or research on behavior problem children. Satisfactory reviews of this literature are already available and should be consulted before undertaking this program (see Dangel & Polster, 1984; Forehand & McMahon, 1981; Mash, Hamerlynck, & Handy, 1976; Mash, Handy, & Hamerlynck, 1976; Patterson, 1982). The manual is instead intended to be a clinical handbook for conducting only the procedures pertinent to this sequence of child management methods.

TYPES OF CHILDREN APPROPRIATE FOR THIS PROGRAM

This program is expressly intended for children who display noncompliant behavior alone or in conjunction with other childhood disorders. These children are often referred to as having "externalizing" or "acting out" disorders that may go under the more specific diagnoses of oppositional disorder, attention deficit disorders, conduct disorders, or even childhood onset pervasive developmental disorder, provided that noncompliant behavior is a primary problem with the children. The program is also quite applicable to mildly mentally retarded children where noncompliance is a problem for parents. As with any clinical procedure, the program was not designed as a blanket method to be applied to all children, regardless of their presenting problems or the concerns of their families. However, portions of the program may be quite valuable for use with mild situational behavior problems in children whose families are being seen for more general parent, marital, or family therapy. In particular, children displaying "acting out" or defiant behaviors as part of adjustment reactions to parental separation or divorce often respond well to the methods in this program. In short, where children are problematic in listening to parental commands or requests, or in adhering to household or neighborhood rules, this program will prove quite effective.

The program was designed for children between 2 and 11 years of age. It is possible to use the program with children as young as 18 months, but its success greatly hinges on the child's level of language development. Children younger than 2 years with delayed language development will respond less successfully to this program, or their families will require greater training time and practice, than children without such delays. Also, the program may be used with 12-year-old children, depending upon their level of social maturity and the severity of their behavior problems. Immature preadolescents with mild to moderate noncompliant behavior can be successfully treated with this program with appropriate modifications accounting for their greater level of mental development and desire to participate in the family's decision-making process concerning their behavior. For children older than 12 years, I strongly recommend the behavioral family therapy program designed by Arthur Robin (1979, 1981, 1984, in press).

The present program has also been successfully employed with single parents, those in low income or educational levels, and even abusive families, although the constraints noted above apply here as well. Even where the child in an abusive family is not noncompliant, this program can serve to provide parents with more humane and effective methods of dealing with the everyday management of a child.

While the program can certainly stand alone, and often does, as the primary form of intervention provided to parents of noncompliant children, it can also serve as a core component to other forms of therapy being provided to troubled parents or families who also happen to have misbehaving children. Many therapists have found the program highly useful as an adjunct to marital counseling where disagreements over child management are an issue in the marriage, or to psychotherapy with anxious, depressed, or otherwise maladjusted adults who are also having problems managing the behavior of their children.

GOALS OF THE PROGRAM

The present program has a limited number of goals but is highly effective at accomplishing them with most families. These are:

1. To improve parental management skills and competence in dealing with child behavior problems, particularly noncompliance.

2. To increase parental knowledge of the causes of childhood misbehavior and the principles and concepts underlying the social learning of such behavior.
3. To improve child compliance to commands and rules given by the parents.

OUTCOMES EXPECTED FROM THIS PROGRAM

The procedures described here have a substantial amount of research supporting their efficacy. However, the degree of success is greatly affected by the extent, nature, and severity of the child's psychopathology and that of the family. With children whose major problem is noncompliance or oppositional behavior and whose families are not seriously dysfunctional, this program usually results in bringing the child's behavior and compliance within the range considered normal for children of that age group. Children with more serious forms of developmental psychopathology, such as attention deficit disorders or childhood onset pervasive developmental disorders, that are chronic in nature, are often improved in their compliance under this program. Nevertheless, many may continue after treatment to be rated as more deviant than normal children on child behavior rating scales. With such children, the attitude taken is one of training parents to cope with the child's problems rather than cure them; yet the program can minimize the extent to which child noncompliance contributes to the child's various problems and the distress within the family.

Children older than 11 or 12 years of age, or those who are seriously aggressive and assaultive with others, should not be considered candidates for this program. They often do not respond, or their reaction to the procedures results in even more distress for the family than existed prior to treatment. Children who have had 11 to 17 years of effectively utilizing coercive behavior, especially that involving physical resistance, are unlikely to be changed by this program. In fact, they may react to its procedures with intolerable rates or intensities of physically aggressive behavior that cannot be handled by the family. Such children are better treated within residential treatment facilities or inpatient child psychiatry units, at the conclusion of which parents can be trained in these procedures to prepare them for the children's return to the home.

Parents with at least a high school education and with minimal degrees of personal or family distress are likely to do quite well in acquiring and utilizing the skills and knowledge taught in this program. They are also more likely to report satisfaction with the procedures. Such parents report not only improved child behavior but also an improved sense of parental competence and better marital and family functioning. Parents with less than average intelligence or with less than a high school education usually do not achieve this same degree of success. However, with greater involvement and training from the therapist and more time for practice, these families can achieve significant improvements in child management. Parents with serious forms of psychopathology (psychosis, severe depression, alcohol/drug dependency, etc.) typically do not respond well in this program. Severe marital discord is also a predictor of failure within this (Forehand & McMahon, 1981) and other (Patterson, 1982) parent training programs. Perhaps it is better to refer such parents for marriage or divorce counseling to help resolve this issue before parent training in child management is offered. In a similar vein, Robert Wahler (Dumas & Wahler, 1983) has also shown that "insular" mothers are less likely to succeed in child management programs than are noninsular mothers. Insularity here refers to the extent to which a mother is isolated from the typical social support networks that exist within the community (e.g., family ties, friendships, recreational activities with others, and church groups). It might be better in such cases to attempt to address the insularity or social isolation before using this parent training program.

ORGANIZATION OF THE MANUAL

This training manual has been organized into three parts. Part 1 provides information on the background of the program, its theoretical and research basis, methods of evaluating noncompliance in children both before and after treatment, and various prerequisite information to consider before undertaking this program of therapy. Part 2 provides detailed instructions on conducting each of the steps of the program. Clinicians may wish not only to acquaint themselves thoroughly with this section but also to review periodically the contents of each step while training families. Each step in this part begins with an outline of the material to be taught in the step, so that a clinician experienced in this program need only refer to this outline during a training session with a family. Part 3 contains materials that are highly useful during the pre- and post-treatment evaluation of the children and their families, as well as the handouts to be used with each step of the program.

SUMMARY

The procedures detailed in this manual are designed specifically for families with children who are noncompliant with commands or rules and who range in age from 2 to 11 years. The methods are for use by experienced clinicians with adequate training in delivering psychological services to disturbed families and their children. Although the procedures are highly effective, their success is dependent upon the nature and severity of the child's problems, the extent and severity of parental and family psychopathology, and the level of parental intelligence and motivation to use these methods. When taught properly, this program can be significantly effective in diminishing or eliminating behavior problems in children.

1
Prerequisite Information for Using the Program

CHAPTER ONE

Rationale for the Program

This chapter presents the primary focus of the parent training program, the rationale behind selecting this focus, and the important findings from research supporting this focus. As Mash and Terdal (1981, 1987) have stated, the target of behavioral assessment and treatment must be clearly defined, have relevance to the presenting complaints of the child and family, have significance for the child's present and future adjustment, and where possible be grounded in an adequate theory of development and maintenance. The target of this intervention program, *child noncompliance*, clearly meets these requirements (Forehand & McMahon, 1981).

NONCOMPLIANCE DEFINED

The term noncompliance as used here will refer to three categories of child behavior.

1. The child fails to initiate requested behaviors within a reasonable time after a command given by an adult. In most cases, a reasonable time refers to 15 seconds after the command was given, although parents may specifically stipulate when compliance is to be initiated (e.g., "As soon as that cartoon is over, pick-up your toys!"). Research on noncompliance has generally used a more stringent interval of 10 seconds as a reasonable time for compliance to be initiated.

2. The child fails to sustain compliance until the requirements stipulated in an adult's command have been fulfilled. Some may consider this behavior category as short attention span or a lack of sustained attention to tasks ("on task" behavior).

3. The child fails to follow previously taught rules of conduct in a situation. Such behaviors as leaving one's desk in class without permission, running off in a department store without permission, stealing, lying, hitting or aggressing against others, taking food from the kitchen without permission, and swearing at one's parents are just a few child behaviors parents consider to be rule violations of previously taught standards of conduct.

Examples of noncompliant behaviors are shown in Table 1.1. Despite their apparent dissimilarity, all of these behaviors can be construed as failures to comply with direct commands or previously stated rules that govern behavior in particular settings. Some of them are in fact direct efforts of the child to escape or avoid the imposition of the command (see Patterson, 1982). Hence, all may be treated by a common program that addresses noncompliance. It is this that distinguishes this parent training program from many others that may single out one or several types of inappropriate behavior but fail to address the general class of noncompliant behaviors.

RATIONALE FOR TREATING NONCOMPLIANCE

This program does not focus simply on child noncompliance, but also on those social processes in the family felt to have developed or sustained the child's noncompliance. These processes are more thoroughly explained below in the section "Causes of Noncompliance in Children." Noncompliance is the most obvious product of these social processes, although there are others of some significance, such as maternal depression, parental stress and low self-esteem, marital discord, and sibling hostility, to name but a few. There are many well-established reasons for choosing noncompliance, and its underlying family processes, as the focus of intervention.

First, noncompliance in various forms appears to be the most frequent complaint of families referring children to child mental health centers (Johnson, Wahl, Martin, & Johansson 1973; Patterson, 1976, 1982). While these children may receive various diagnoses of oppositional disorder, conduct disorders, attention deficit disorders,

Table 1.1. Types of Noncompliant Behaviors Common in Children Referred for Behavior Disorders

Yells	Steals	Physically resists
Whines	Lies	Destroys property
Complains	Argues	Physically fights with others
Defies	Humiliates	Fails to complete school home-
Screams	Teases	work
Throws tantrums	Ignores requests	Disrupts others' activities
Throws objects	Runs off	Ignores self-help tasks
Talks back	Cries	
Swears	Fails to complete chores	

adjustment reactions, and so forth, a major concern of the parents or teachers referring such a child is his or her inability to comply with directions, commands, rules, or codes of social conduct appropriate to the child's age group. Parents may complain that the child fails to listen, throws temper tantrums, is aggressive or destructive, is verbally oppositional or resistant to authority, fails to do homework, does not adequately perform chores, cannot play appropriately with neighborhood children, lies or steals frequently, or behaves inappropriately in other ways. However, all of these behaviors are violations of commands, directions, or rules that were either previously stated to the child or are directly stated in the particular situation. Hence, noncompliance, broadly defined, encompasses the majority of acting out, externalizing, or conduct problem forms of behavior.

Second, noncompliance underlies the majority of negative interactions between family members and the referred child. Patterson (1976, 1982) and others (see Forehand & McMahon, 1981) have shown that disruptive or aggressive behavior from children does not occur continuously or randomly throughout the day but instead appears in "bursts" or "chunks." These are episodes of high-rate, often intense periods of oppositional or coercive behavior by the child that punctuate an otherwise normal stream of behavior. Research suggests that one of the most common precipitators of child noncompliance is parental or teacher commands or requests.

Such negative encounters between adult and child appear to take the form shown schematically in Figure 1.1. The sequence is initiated by the command given by a parent, perhaps to have the child pick up his or her toys. On rare occasions, the behavior disordered child may

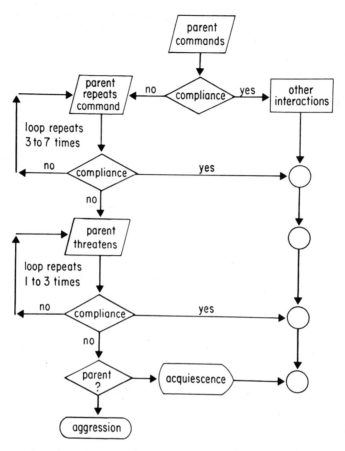

Figure 1.1. Flow chart showing possible sequences of interactions between parent and child during a command-compliance encounter. From *Hyperactive Children: A Handbook for Diagnosis and Treatment* (p. 100) by R. A. Barkley, 1981, New York: Guilford Press. Copyright 1981 by Guilford Press. Reprinted by permission.

obey this first request. This usually occurs where the commands involve some very brief amount of effort or work from the child (e.g., "Please hand me a Kleenex.") or involve an activity that is pleasurable to the child or that may promise immediate reinforcement for compliance (e.g., "Get in the car so we can go get some ice cream."). In these instances, as shown on the right side of Figure 1.1, the child complies with the request, and the family proceeds into other interactions. This may not seem especially important, but what is significant here is that rarely is such compliance followed by a positive reaction from the parent, such as acknowledging appreciation for the compliance. When such compliance goes unnoted by parents, it frequently declines in occurrence over time and may eventually only occur where the activity requested involves something intrinsically highly rewarding and immediately available to the child. In such cases the child obeys not because of previous reinforcement by the parent for doing so but because the specific activity required of the child is itself highly reinforcing.

It is often only in a minority of instances that behavior disordered children will comply with the first commands or requests of parents. More often, the pattern of events is that seen on the left side of Figure 1.1. Here the child has failed to comply with the initial command, which is often followed by the parent's simply repeating the command to the child. This is rarely met with compliance from the child, and so the command may be repeated, over and over perhaps as many as 3 to 7 times (or more!) in various forms, without the child complying with any of the commands. At some point, parental frustration arises, and the emotional intensity of the interaction heightens. The parent may then issue a warning or threat, that if compliance does not occur, something unpleasant or punitive will follow. Yet the child often fails to comply with the threat, in part, perhaps, because the parents frequently repeat it. Over time, both parent and child escalate in their level of emotional behavior toward the other, with voices rising in volume as well as intensity and with collateral behavioral displays of anger, defiance, or destructiveness.

The interaction sequence ends in one of several ways. Sometimes the parent disciplines the child, perhaps by sending the child to his or her room, removing a favored privilege from the child, or spanking the child. More often the parent acquiesces, and the command is left uncompleted or only partially completed by the child. Even if the task is eventually done, however, the child has succeeded in at least delaying its completion, allowing greater time for play or some other desired activity.

This eventual child compliance may prove quite an enigma to parents and therapists alike. That is, parents may believe that they have actually "won," or succeeded in getting the child to listen, yet they are surprised to find that the child will again attempt to avoid or defy that same command when issued later. Parents may question the therapist as to why the child continues to misbehave or defy them when he or she ultimately will be forced to perform the task. The key to understanding this situation is to see it from a child's point of view rather than an adult's. Adults tend to look at this situation in its entirety and are able to see that ultimately they will always make the child perform this command (e.g., get ready for bed). Most children will not show this breadth of awareness of the entire interaction sequence but will simply view it as a moment-to-moment interaction with their parents in which the child's immediate goal is to escape or avoid doing the requested task. As a result, every minute the child is able to procrastinate is an additional minute to continue doing what he or she was doing prior to the imposition of the command—an activity often more reinforcing to the child than what the parents may wish him or her to do. It is also an additional minute of avoiding the often unpleasant task requested by the parent.

This may help to explain why parents are often puzzled that the child spends more time avoiding the requested task, as well as arguing or defying the parents, than it would have taken to do it. The moment-by-moment procrastination of the child is doubly reinforcing, serving to permit continued participation in a desired activity (positive reinforcement) while, for the moment, successfully avoiding the unpleasant task being imposed by the parent (negative reinforcement). The outcome of the interaction (eventual punishment or forced compliance) is sufficiently delayed so as to have little, if any, influence on the child's immediate behavior.

Acquiescence occurs when the child fails to accomplish the requested activity. In some instances, the child leaves the situation. He or she may run out of the room or yard without accomplishing the task. Or the parent may storm out of the room in anger or frustration, leaving the child to return to the previous activities. In some cases, parents may complete the command themselves, as is seen when a parent picks up the toys for or with the child, after directing the child to do so. In a few instances, the child may not only succeed in escaping from doing the task but also receive some positive consequence in addition. This can be seen where parents direct children to pick up toys, for example, and the children refuse, throw themselves down, and hit their heads against the floor. A parent may respond to this behavioral display, out of fear that the child may be injured, by picking the child up and holding him or her in the parent's lap while trying to soothe the child's feelings. As a result, the child's tantrum and self-injurious behavior are not only negatively reinforced by escaping from the unpleasant task initially requested by the parent, but also positively reinforced by the attention from the parent. It is likely that such dual consequences for oppositional behavior by children rapidly accelerate the acquisition and maintenance of such behavior patterns in future similar circumstances (Patterson, 1976). These acquiescent interaction patterns can be found to underlie many of the negative encounters between parents and behavior disordered children. They must be the focus of treatment if the complaints of the family are to be ameliorated.

A third rationale for selecting noncompliance as the target of intervention is its pervasiveness, greater than that of other behavioral problems seen in children. Research (Forehand & McMahon, 1981; Patterson, 1982) suggests that children who display noncompliance or coercive behavior in one situation are highly likely to employ it elsewhere, with other commands or instructions and with other adults or children. Improving child compliance may therefore have more widespread effects across many situations and individuals than would be seen had a behavioral problem specific to only one situation been selected as the focus of therapy.

Fourth, a child's noncompliant behavior, as outlined in Figure 1.1, may have indirect effects on family functioning that may, in a reciprocal fashion, come to have further detrimental effects on the psychological adjustment of the behavior disordered child. As noted already, the child rapidly acquires a set of coercive behaviors to use against the parent and other family members or even peers, when the child is instructed to do something he or she does not like to do. Parents may also come to acquire a set of rapidly escalating coercive behaviors to use with the child because of those rare occasions where yelling, threatening, or punishing the child has eventually led to compliance. Furthermore, over time parents may come to give progressively fewer commands to the child, knowing in advance they will be met with resistant, oppositional behavior by the child. Parents instead may assume more of the child's chores and responsibilities or assign them to a more compliant sibling. The latter situation may then lead to siblings developing hostility and resentment toward the behavior disordered child because the problem child has comparatively less work to do. In other cases, parents and siblings come to spend progressively less leisure time and initiate fewer recreational pursuits with the behavior disordered child so as to avoid any further unpleasantries with that child. The effects such patterns within a family might have on one's self-esteem as a parent, on marital harmony should the child oppose one parent more than the other, or on the self-esteem of the behavior disordered child almost goes without saying.

Fifth, noncompliance in children appears to be a significant predictor of later maladjustment during the adolescent and young adult years. That is, noncompliant and coercive behavior that is of such magnitude and duration that it leads to referral for mental health services significantly predicts later problems with academic performance, conduct problems, delinquency, and peer acceptance (Wells & Forehand, 1985). Research is coming to show that the presence of conduct problems in children is strongly associated with greater maladjustment in adolescence than are many other forms of deviant child behavior (Paternite & Loney, 1980; Patterson, 1982). Noncompliance is therefore singled out for treatment because of the possible future consequences to the child if left untreated.

Finally, it would be hard to undertake the treatment of any other presenting problems of a child without first addressing the child's noncompliance. For example, attempting to toilet train a 3-year-old noncompliant child is not likely to prove successful until the child is taught to comply with requests. This will also be true of noncompliant children who must follow other medical or educational programs; such programs will likely have little success until compliance with adult instructions is developed.

IMPORTANT ASPECTS OF DEVIANT PARENT-CHILD INTERACTIONS

The substantial body of research on the parent–child relations in families with behavior problem children is too great to review here. However, the findings from this research are important to consider in the clinical training of these families and are summarized briefly below.

It appears that parents of behavior problem children at times provide positive consequences to children for their deviant behavior, which only serves to increase and sustain its occurrence in future interactions. When children act out, throw temper tantrums, or directly oppose commands, it is difficult not to attend to such behavior. Even though such attention may seem negative to the parents, it may still serve to increase future oppositional behavior, as even negative parental attention can serve as a reinforcer to a child who otherwise gets minimal family attention. On other occasions, parents may provide positive attention or rewards to children in an effort to get them to stop "making a scene" in a store, restaurant, or other public places. Buying a child the candy bar for which he or she has been throwing a tantrum is but one obvious way in which parents may accelerate the acquisition and maintenance of deviant child behavior.

Conversely, parents may provide less attention or reinforcement to prosocial or appropriate behaviors of the child. Clinical experience suggests that parents of deviant children may monitor or survey child behaviors less often than parents of normal children, so that they may not always be aware of ongoing appropriate child behaviors. Even if they are aware that the child is behaving well, they may elect not to attend or give praise to the child for several reasons. One is that many parents report that when they praise or attend to good behavior in their child it only serves to provoke a burst of negative behavior from the child. This leads the parent to adopt the attitude of "let sleeping dogs lie" when they encounter ongoing acceptable child behavior. It has not been established that this reaction occurs when parents have tried to praise a behavior problem child or, if it does, what the learning history was that established this behavioral pattern. It is possible that parental praise for good behavior in a child prompts the child to misbehave because the child continues to receive parental attention for bad behavior. Had the child continued to behave well, the parent might have terminated the interaction, moving on to do something else. Another reason parents may fail to react positively when a deviant child behaves well is that parents dislike interacting with the problematic child and will choose to avoid such interaction when possible. Parents of chronically deviant children often develop animosity or grudges toward the child, so that they will elect not to give praise when the child finally behaves well. This may eventually lead to parents' spending significantly less leisure and recreational time with the deviant child simply because it is not fun to do so.

Parents of behavior problem children may also monitor or attend less to unacceptable behavior so as to avoid further confrontations with the child. As in the saying "out of sight, out of mind," parents may eventually reduce the amount of effort they spend monitoring a child's ongoing behavior within the home so as not to have to confront any minor unacceptable behavior that may be occurring. By overlooking the problem behavior, they do not have to face another negative, coercive exchange with the child about the matter. This may explain the frequent clinical observation that such parents seem to be oblivious to ongoing negative behavior occurring in their presence—behavior other parents would normally react to in a corrective fashion. Such a decline in parental monitoring of child conduct is also associated with the development of a more serious form of conduct disorder that involves covert antisocial behavior, such as lying, stealing, or destruction of community property (Patterson, 1982).

Parents may actually punish prosocial or appropriate behavior at times, again because of possible resentment that may have developed over years of negative interactions with the child. Parents may often give "back-handed compliments" to a child for finally doing something correctly, as when they sarcastically remark, "It's about time you cleaned your room; why couldn't you do that yesterday?" For all of these reasons, parents are simply not providing appropriate consequences that would be expected to manage or control ongoing child behavior effectively.

Patterson (1976, 1982) has theorized that both parents and children in families with behavior disordered children are negatively reinforced for behaving in aggressive and coercive ways toward each other. He proposes that this may explain why parents and children, once having begun a negative interaction with each other, will escalate this negative behavior very quickly to intense levels of aggression or coercion. Furthermore, the likelihood that such forms of interaction will occur again is greatly increased as a result. This theory has substantial research support and is worth understanding by clinical practitioners.

It is first necessary to remember that negative reinforcement is *not* the same as punishment—a mistake often made by those less experienced in behavioral terminology. Negative reinforcement is said to occur when, in a situation where the child is subjected to aversive, unpleasant, or otherwise negative stimuli, the child behaves in a way that successfully terminates the ongoing aversive situation or permits escape in the future from such situations. For instance, when the parent attempts to impose the command of getting ready for bed while the child is watching a favorite television program, the child often finds this imposition to be aversive. The child may oppose, resist, or otherwise escape from the parental request through aggressive or coercive behavior that delays having to get ready for bed. The child's success at escaping from the command, even if only temporarily, negatively reinforces the oppositional behavior. The next time the parent asks the child to get ready for bed, the likelihood of the child resisting the command has increased. The more a parent persists at repeating the request, the more intense the child's resistance may become because of this previous success at escaping or avoiding the activity specified in the command. As already noted above, many parents may eventually acquiesce to this type of coercive behavior. Parents need not acquiesce to every command for a child to acquire resistant behavior.

Parents may also acquire aggressive or coercive behavior toward their behavior disordered child by much the same process. In this case, the parent may have been successful at getting a child to cease whining, refusing, or throwing tantrums and to comply with a command through the parent's use of yelling, screaming, or even physical aggression against the child. The parent may also have discovered that rapidly increasing the intensity of negative behavior toward the child is more successful at getting the child to obey, especially if the child initially opposes the command. In subsequent situations the parent may escalate very quickly to intense negative behavior toward a child because of a history of success at terminating oppositional child behavior. The parent need not be successful with this strategy every time the parent confronts oppositional behavior. Only occasional success with coercive behavior is needed to sustain this type of behavior in parents.

Viewed from this perspective, both parent and child have a prior history of partial success at escaping or avoiding each other's aversive or coercive behavior. As a result, each will continue to employ it with the other in most negative interactions. Over time, each learns that when a command–compliance situation arises, the faster each escalates the intensity and coerciveness, the more likely the other is to acquiesce to the demands. As a result, confronting interactions between parent and child may escalate quickly to quite intense, emotional, and even aggressive confrontations, which, on some occasions, may end with physical abuse of the child by the parent, destruction of property by the child, or assault against the parent.

This view also implies that much deviant child behavior is not sustained by positive attention or reinforcement from the parent. Accordingly, when a clinician tells such a parent to ignore deviant child behavior, it may only worsen the problem, as it is likely to be viewed by the child as acquiescence. In many cases, parents cannot ignore the child because in so doing the child escapes from performing the command given by the parent. Parents in such a situation will have to continue interacting with the child if they wish to get the task accomplished. Many experienced clinicians have noted this problem in training parents of behavior problem children—ignoring deviant behavior is not always successful nor possible. Instead, a great deal of negative child behavior is developed through escape/ avoidance learning (negative reinforcement) and is maintained because of its success in avoiding unpleasant activities often invoked by parents. As Patterson (1982) suggests, and as this program teaches, mild punishment (usually time out from reinforcement) must be incorporated into the parent training program if it is to be successful at diminishing child noncompliance that has developed through negative reinforcement.

Patterson has also noted (1976) that parents are likely, once trained, to rely predominantly upon the punishment methods taught in the program and to diminish their use of positive reinforcement methods. Therapists must anticipate this parental regression and address it during the last few sessions of parent training as well as during follow-up booster sessions. Parents must be instructed that most punishment methods lose their effectiveness when they are relied upon as the primary management technique with children and when sufficient positive reinforcement methods are not provided for the alternative, appropriate behavior desired from the child.

This review of several important aspects of deviant parent-child interactions has a number of implications for the training of such parents in effective child management procedures, the most important of which are that parents must be trained to (1) increase the value of their attention and its worth in changing their child's behavior; (2) increase the positive attention and incentives they provide for compliance while decreasing the inadvertent punishment they provide for occasional compliance; (3) decrease the amount of inadvertent positive attention they provide to negative child behavior; (4) increase the use of immediate mild punishment for occurrences of child noncompliance; (5) reduce the frequency of repeat commands they employ; (6) recognize and rapidly terminate escalating and confronting negative interactions with the child; and (7) insure that they do not regress to a predominantly punitive child management strategy once training has been completed.

CAUSES OF NONCOMPLIANCE IN CHILDREN

As discussed above, one of the major causes of noncompliance is ineffective child management methods being employed by parents. As a result, noncompliance by children becomes a very effective method for escaping or avoiding unpleasant, boring, or effortful tasks and on some occasions even getting rewards for doing so (e.g., candy for the tantrum in the store). But it would be erroneous to conclude from this that all noncompliant behavior is simply learned. While the exact form, nature, or topography of the noncompliant responses from a child probably has much to do with his or her learning history within a family, the probability of acquiring or emitting noncompliance is also affected by other factors.

First, it is becoming clear that children having certain temperaments and cognitive characteristics are more prone to emit coercive-aggressive behavior and acquire noncompliance than are other children. Children who are easily prone to emotional responses, are often irritable, have poor habit regulation, are highly active, and/or are more inattentive and impulsive appear more likely to acquire noncompliance and coercion than are children not having such negative temperamental characteristics. Overactivity, inattention, and impulsivity are more likely to prevent a child from finishing assigned activities and thus more likely to elicit increased commands, supervision, and negative reactions from parents. Such children may also be more likely to respond to these reprimands and parental confrontations with negative emotional reactions. If such reactions are successful at eliminating further demands, their use following subsequent commands by parents will be increased and sustained.

Second, noncompliance in a child may also increase in probability because of similar temperamental and cognitive characteristics in the child's parents. Immature, inexperienced, impulsive, inattentive, or temperamental parents may display inconsistent management strategies with a deviant child. This permits periodic success by the child at avoiding demands, further reinforcing the child's use of oppositional or coercive behavior. Such parents may also employ coercive behavior with others in the family, providing a model of such behavior for the child to imitate.

Finally, it is also possible that frequent or chronic stress events within a family create such inconsistency in child management methods by parents that the children are further predisposed to develop or sustain noncompliance within family interactions. It is all too common for many families referred for treatment of a deviant child to have most or all of these predisposing characteristics: temperamental, impulsive, active, and inattentive children being raised by immature, temperamental, and impulsive parents within a family experiencing greater marital, financial, health, and personal distress in its members.

SUMMARY

This chapter has described the importance of focusing upon child noncompliance as the major target of the parent training program. The process whereby children may develop, maintain, or increase their rate of oppositional, defiant, or noncompliant behavior was discussed in some detail, and it appears that such behavior is chiefly sustained by its usefulness for escaping or avoiding generally unpleasant, effortful, or boring tasks assigned by parents and for permitting the child to continue his or her previous activity. It was shown that parents may also come to escalate their rates of negative behavior toward the child because of its occasional success at terminating ongoing unpleasant child behavior, such as tantrums or defiance, and getting eventual child compliance. Both parents and children may be more predisposed toward such types of coercive behavior by virtue of their particular profile of temperamental reactions as well as stress events within the family.

CHAPTER TWO

Assessment Methods
in Parent Training

This chapter will briefly discuss methods used to evaluate noncompliance in children. Although many methods exist for clinically assessing noncompliant children, only that approach used by the author will receive attention here. Other methods are discussed in the texts by Mash and Terdal (1981, 1987), Barkley (1981), Forehand and McMahon (1981), Dangel and Polster (1984), Cairns (1979), and Patterson (1982), as well as in the series *Advances in the Behavioral Assessment of Children and Families* edited by Prinz (e.g., 1986). The methods to be discussed here include the initial interviews with parent and child, rating scales completed by parents and teachers, and direct observational methods for recording parent-child interactions.

INITIAL INTERVIEW

The initial interview with parents will necessarily focus upon the reasons for the child's referral, the specific nature of the problems, their frequency, intensity, and history, as well as the manner in which the parents, and other professionals if prior treatment was received, have attempted to deal with them. You should then conduct a general review of the child's developmental competencies and weaknesses, beginning with a discussion of whether the child manifests delays or deficits in sensory or motor abilities. The interview progresses to possible speech and language problems, and thinking disorders (e.g., tangential rambling of ideas, loose associations, odd or bizarre fascinations, preoccupations or obsessions, and irrelevant responses to questions by others). Thereafter, you should inquire about potentially inappropriate or exaggerated emotional behaviors, such as crying, sadness, or depression; anger, hostility, or rage; excitement, giddiness, hysteria, or mania; and fears, anxieties, aversions, or phobias. A discussion of deviant, immature, or delayed social skills and conduct should follow, including participation in organized clubs, sporting activities, or other social groups. Types and number of friendships and possible difficulties in initiating or sustaining friendships should be briefly discussed. You should review any disturbances in habit patterns, such as sleeping (e.g., insomnia, frequent night waking, early waking, or nightmares or terrors), eating (e.g., overeating, fussy eating, or disturbed dietary preferences), or elimination (e.g., enuresis or encopresis). Finally, existent or past significant medical disorders, somatic complaints, accidents or injuries, or developmental disabilities should be discussed.

You will then want to review the child's developmental history from birth to the present, focusing chiefly upon when the child acquired significant developmental milestones (e.g., walking, speech, and toilet training) and whether significant medical problems were noted at any stage of development. As part of this, you should review the child's history of school performance, inquiring in detail about any performance problems that may have occurred in any grade in school (e.g., underachievement, learning disabilities, special educational assistance, or retention in grade).

It is important to review briefly the family and parental history. I typically begin with a discussion of the length and number of marriages of the parents, the current degree of integrity and stability of the marriage, and reasons for previous separations or divorces, if any. The psychiatric and educational history of each parent is then briefly reviewed for any serious disorders or current conditions that may affect child rearing or parent–child relations. You should also specifically inquire about possible financial, employment, religious, medical, or other stressors in the immediate family, including possible disruptive relations with relatives with whom the parents may frequently interact. Possible psychiatric, emotional, learning, or developmental disorders in siblings should then be briefly discussed, followed by a summary by the parents of the referred child's relationship to each family member. It should be clear from the previous chapter that such areas deserve inquiry, as they will have a direct bearing on the child's management by the parents as well as their motivation for and likely success in training.

Once you have completed this general clinical interview, time should be taken to assess in detail the types of noncompliant interactions existing between the parent and behavior disordered child. This assessment takes the form of a parental interview concerning settings where noncompliance by the child exists, the completion of several child behavior rating scales by the parent (and teachers of school-age children), and the direct observation of parent–child interactions where resources permit. Should this evaluation reveal significant levels of disruptive, noncompliant, or defiant behavior in the child, parent training in child behavior management in this program would be clearly warranted.

PARENT-CHILD INTERACTION INTERVIEW

This interview format was initially developed by Constance Hanf at the University of Oregon Health Sciences Center. Its structure is set forth in Table 2.1. Essentially, you should begin by questioning parents concerning their view of the general interactions they have with the child. This is followed by questions concerning a number of specific situations in which parents and children may experience conflicts with each other. In each situation, should the parent report behavior problems of the child, you follow up with questions 2 through 8 as noted in Table 2.1. These questions are designed to obtain briefly more specific information about the nature of the problematic interaction in that setting. Parents are then asked to rate the perceived severity of the problem interaction on a scale of 1 (mild) to 9 (severe) before proceeding to the next situation in the interview.

Such an interview takes 30 to 45 minutes because of the numerous settings in which noncompliant child behavior occurs. The interview yields valuable information on how parents now manage noncompliance and what must be changed to improve their management

Table 2.1. Parental Interview Format for Assessing Child Misbehavior and Non-compliance

Situations to be discussed with parents	*Follow-up questions for each problem situation*
General—Overall interactions Playing alone Playing with other children Mealtimes Getting dressed/undressed Washing and bathing When parent is on telephone Watching television When visitors are in your home When you are visiting someone's home In public places (stores, restaurants, church, etc.) When parent is occupied with chores When father is home When asked to to chores When asked to do homework When with a babysitter Other situations (in car, at bedtime etc.)	1. Is this a problem area? If so, then proceed with questions 2 to 9. 2. What does the child do in this situation that bothers you? 3. What is your response? 4. What will the child do next? 5. If the problem continues, what will you do next? 6. What is usually the outcome of this interaction? 7. How often do these problems occur in this situation? 8. How do you feel about these problems? 9. On a scale of 1 (no problem) to 9 (severe problem), how severe is this problem for you?

Note. Adapted from an interview format used by C. Hanf, University of Oregon Health Sciences, 1976. From "Hyperactivity" by R. Barkley in *Behavioral Assessment of Childhood Disorders* (p. 148) edited by E. J. Mash and L. G. Terdal, 1981, New York: The Guilford Press. Copyright 1981 by The Guilford Press. Reprinted by permission.

tactics. It can also be repeated at the conclusion of the parent training course to assess improvement in the child from treatment. A blank form for this interview is provided in Part 3 of this manual.

PARENT RATING SCALES OF BEHAVIOR PROBLEMS IN CHILDREN

Where examiner time and caseload preclude such an extensive interview in addition to the typical clinical assessment, a rating scale has been devised to abbreviate the essential information obtained by the interview. This rating scale is the Home Situations Questionnaire

(HSQ), which is provided in Part 3. It contains similar situations as are in the parental interview discussed above and requests parents to indicate whether or not a situation is a problem for them with their child. If so, the parent rates the severity of the problem on a scale from 1 (mild) to 9 (severe). The examiner can then select the worst two of these situations and query the parent, using the seven follow-up questions shown in Table 2.1. Although this method certainly misses some information about the parent–child interaction patterns, it serves as an adequate substitute where circumstances do not permit the more lengthy interview format. The examiner can obtain two scores from the scale, these being the number of problem settings (number of yes answers circled) and the mean severity score (the sum of the severity score numerals circled divided by the total number circled). The scale can also be administered periodically throughout training or at the conclusion of training to assess change in these problem situations.

Normative data and a review of research on its psychometric properties are provided in the paper by Barkley and Edelbrock (1987). These norms are summarized in Table 2.2 by age and sex of the child. The advantage of this scale, however, is not so much to serve as a comparison with normal children as to measure change in the initial problem areas as a function of treatment. The scale has been shown to be sensitive to stimulant-drug effects (Barkley, Karlsson, Strzelecki, & Murphy, 1984), to discriminate behavior-problem from normal children (Barkley, 1981), and to be sensitive to effects from this parent training program (Pollard, Ward, & Barkley, 1983).

Table 2.2. Norms for the Home Situations Questionnaire

Age groups (in years)	n	Number of problem settings	Mean severity
Boys			
4–5	162	3.1 (2.8)	1.7 (1.4)
6–8	205	4.1 (3.3)	2.0 (1.4)
9–11	138	3.6 (3.3)	1.9 (1.5)
Girls			
4–5	146	2.2 (2.6)	1.3 (1.4)
6–8	202	3.4 (3.5)	1.6 (1.5)
9–11	142	2.7 (3.2)	1.4 (1.4)

Note. Table entries are means with standard deviations in parentheses. Reprinted with permission from Michael J. Breen, Ph.D.

Declines in the score of mean severity of problem behavior on this scale as a function of this parent training program are shown graphically in Figure 2.1, taken from the study by Pollard et al. (1983).

Another scale of value in assessing child conduct problems is the Child Behavior Checklist (CBCL; Achenbach & Edelbrock, 1983). This 113-item questionnaire, to be completed by parents, concerns most of the complaints made by parents of children referred to child guidance centers. The scale comprises two parts; the first deals with adaptive functioning and assesses the child's degree of participation in social organizations, sports, clubs, household chores, hobbies, and friendships, as well as relationships with siblings. The second part deals with behavior problems. These 113 items are scored to yield eight or nine (depending on age) factor scales (e.g., Depression, Obsessive-Compulsive, Hyperactive, Aggressive, and Delinquent), which can be compared to a sample of normal children to evaluate the extent of deviance of these parental ratings. Those factor scales dealing with conduct problems are most useful for the purpose of evaluating child noncompliance. The CBCL is useful for ages 4 to 16 years as a global screening instrument for most common forms of child psychopathology (Barkley, 1987). The Child Behavior Checklist can be obtained from Thomas Achenbach, Ph.D., Child and Adolescent Psychiatry, Department of Psychiatry, University of Vermont, 5 South Prospect St., Burlington, VT 05401.

A shorter scale that predominantly assesses conduct problems and is also of value in a noncompliance evaluation is the Conners Parent's Questionnaire. This is a 48-item questionnaire concerning various types of child behavior problems. The scale can be scored to yield five factors: Conduct Problems, Learning Problems, Psychosomatic Problems, Impulsity–Hyperactivity, and Anxiety. The norms and scoring instructions are provided in Table 2.3 (Goyette, Conners, & Ulrich, 1978). This parent's questionnaire is provided in Part 3 of this manual. The scale can be used both before and after treatment to assess declines in child behavior problems as a function of parent training in child management skills. Such declines were demonstrated in a study by Pollard et al. (1983), which employed this parent training program. The results are displayed in Figure 2.2, and show a progressive decline in parent ratings on this scale over the course of parent training with these three children with attention deficit disorders (ADD) and conduct problems. Nevertheless, the ratings for these boys remained toward the high end of the normal range after

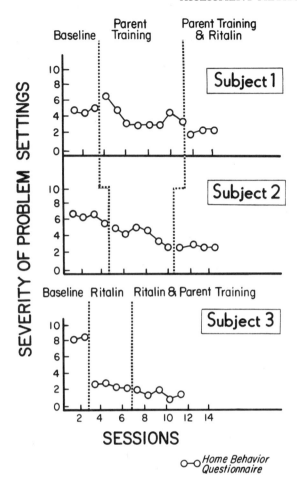

Figure 2.1. Mean severity ratings of behavior problem situations from the Home Situations Questionnaire, for three children with attention deficit disorders across three treatment conditions: Baseline (no treatment), parent training in child management skills, and parent training and Ritalin. From "The Effects of Parent Training and Ritalin on the Parent-Child Interactions of Hyperactive Boys" by S. Pollard, E. Ward, and R. Barkley, 1983, *Child and Family Behavior Therapy, 5,* p. 63. Copyright 1983 by Haworth Press. Reprinted with permission.

treatment was terminated, underscoring the point made earlier that parents of ADD children must be prepared to cope with, rather than cure, the behavioral problems of their children. However, noncompliance in these children was greatly diminished compared to pretreatment levels. It should be noted that the addition of Ritalin, a

Table 2.3. Category (Factor) Norms for the Conners Parent's Questionnaire

Age (years)	n^a	(I) Conduct Problems		(II) Learning problems		(III) Psychosomatic problems		(IV) Impulsivity–hyperactivity		(V) Anxiety		Hyperactivity index	
		$\bar{x}$	SD	$\bar{x}$	SD	$\bar{x}$	SD	$\bar{x}$	SD	$\bar{x}$	SD	$\bar{x}$	SD
Males by age													
3–5	45	.53	.39	.50	.33	.07	.15	1.01	.65	.67	.61	.72	.40
6–8	76	.50	.40	.64	.45	.13	.23	.93	.60	.51	.51	.69	.46
9–11	73	.53	.38	.54	.52	.18	.26	.92	.60	.42	.47	.66	.44
12–14	59	.49	.41	.66	.57	.22	.44	.82	.54	.58	.59	.62	.45
15–17	38	.47	.44	.62	.55	.13	.26	.70	.51	.59	.58	.51	.41
Females by age													
3–5	29	.49	.35	.62	.57	.10	.17	1.15	.77	.51	.59	.78	.56
6–8	57	.41	.28	.45	.38	.19	.27	.95	.59	.57	.66	.59	.35
9–11	55	.40	.36	.43	.38	.17	.28	.80	.59	.49	.57	.52	.34
12–14	63	.39	.40	.44	.45	.23	.28	.72	.55	.54	.53	.49	.34
15–17	34	.37	.33	.35	.38	.19	.25	.60	.55	.51	.53	.42	.34

Note. The norms are taken from "Normative Data on Revised Conners Parent and Teacher Rating Scales" by C. H. Goyette, C. K. Conners, and R. F. Ulrich, 1978, Journal of Abnormal Child Psychology, 6, p. 231. Copyright 1978 by Plenum Publishing Corp. Reprinted by permission. The scores are derived by assigning 0, 1, 2, and 3 points to the anwers "not at all," "just a little," "pretty much," and "very much," respectively, for each item. The scores for these items assigned to each factor are then summed and divided by the number of questions assigned to or loading on that factor. The items assigned to each factor from the Conners Parent's Questionnaire are as follows: Conduct Problems: questions 2, 8, 14, 19, 20, 21, 22, 23, 27, 33, 34, and 39; Learning Problem: questions 10, 25, 31, and 37; Psychosomatic Problems: questions 32, 41, 43, 44, and 48; Impulsivity-Hyperactivity: questions 4, 5, 11, and 13; Anxiety: questions 12, 16, 24, and 47; Hyperactivity index: questions 4, 7, 11, 13, 14, 25, 31, 33, 37, and 38.

$^a n$ = number of subjects per age group.

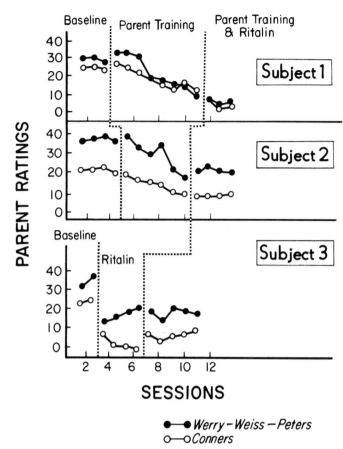

Figure 2.2. Parent ratings of child behavior problems on the Conners Parent Rating Scale (Revised) and the Werry-Weiss-Peters Activity Rating Scale for three children with attention deficit disorders across three treatment conditions: baseline (no treatment), parent training in child management skills, and parent training and Ritalin. From "The Effects of Parent Training and Ritalin on the Parent-Child Interactions of Hyperactive Boys" by S. Pollard, E. Ward, and R. Barkley, 1983, *Child and Family Behavior Therapy, 5,* p. 62. Copyright 1983 by Haworth Press. Reprinted with permission.

stimulant drug commonly used with ADD children, did little to further improve these parent ratings of child behavior beyond those reductions already achieved by the parent training program.

PARENT SELF-REPORT SCALES OF DEPRESSION AND MARITAL DISCORD

As already noted, the extent of parental depression and marital discord in a family directly affects the degree of noncompliance in children referred for behavior disorders and the success of their parents in such a parent training program. Two brief screening scales of these parental problems are available for conveniently assessing the parents of clinic-referred children. The Beck Depression Scale (Beck, 1967) is a 21-item multiple-choice questionnaire designed to permit a brief assessment of self-reported levels of depression in the respondent. It is available from The Psychological Corporation, 555 Academic Court, San Antonio, TX 78204-9990. The Locke-Wallace Marital Adjustment Test (Locke & Wallace, 1959) is a brief 19-item multiple-choice questionnaire for evaluating levels of marital discord in a family. This scale can be obtained from Harvey J. Locke, 975 Calle Angosta, Thousand Oaks, CA 91360.

TEACHER RATINGS OF CHILD BEHAVIOR

The child's primary teacher(s) should be mailed a packet of rating scales to complete and return. It is best to do this before the child's clinic appointment so as to have the information available to discuss with the child's parents. This packet should include

   1. Child Behavior Checklist—Teacher Report Form (Achenbach & Edelbrock, 1983). This questionnaire has two sections, the first dealing with adaptive functioning at school and the second with behavior problems. The adaptive functioning section can be scored for five scales (school performance, working hard, behaving appropriately, learning, and happy) or two summary scores, one for school performance and the second for total adaptive functioning (sum of remaining four scales). The behavior problem scale has 113 items worded similarly to the parent report form described above. Norms are available for two age groups (6 to 11 and 12 to 16 years) for each sex. The scales for 6- to 11-year-old boys are: anxious, social-withdrawal, unpopular, self-destructive, obsessive-compulsive, inattentive, nervous-overactive, and aggressive. This scale can be obtained from Thomas Achenbach, Ph.D., at the address given above for the CBCL.

2. Conners Teacher's Questionnaire. The Teacher's Questionnaire is a 28-item questionnaire constructed similarly to the Parent's Questionnaire described above. The factors are Conduct Problems, Hyperactivity, and Inattention-Passivity. The scale generally assesses conduct problems and noncompliance in the school environment. It is provided in Part 3 of this manual. The norms and scoring instructions are provided in Table 2.4 (Goyette et al., 1978).

3. School Situations Questionnaire (SSQ; Barkley, 1981). This rating scale is similar to the HSQ except that the settings to be rated deal with school situations most likely to be problematic for clinic-referred children. The scale lists 12 situations (e.g., during individual desk work, in the hallways, during small group work), and the teacher is asked to indicate whether or not the child is a problem in each. If so, the teacher rates the problem on a scale from 1 (mild) to 9 (severe). Two scores are derived, the number of problem settings and their mean severity rating. The scale is provided in Part 3 of this manual, and the norms by age and sex of children are set forth in Table 2.5.

DIRECT OBSERVATION OF NONCOMPLIANCE

Several coding systems are available for recording parent-child interactions. Probably the most complex of these is that used by Patterson (1982) in his extensive research on families with aggressive children. The system requires a lengthy training period and yields far more information than is needed in clinical circumstances. Other such systems are those used by Wahler (1975) and Mash, Terdal, & Anderson (1973; see Barkley, 1981), but again training time to use the system is somewhat lengthy, and the system captures information on far more than parent command-child noncompliance interactions.

A relatively simple system to learn and implement in clinical situations is that used by Forehand and McMahon (1981), which was expressly designed for recording noncompliance in parent-child in-

Table 2.4. Norms for the Conners Teacher's Questionnaire

Age (years)	n^a	(I) Conduct problems		(II) Hyperactivity		(III) Inattention-passivity		Hyperactivity index	
		$\bar{x}$	SD	$\bar{x}$	SD	$\bar{x}$	SD	$\bar{x}$	SD
Males by age									
3-5	13	.45	.80	.79	.89	.92	1.00	.81	.96
6-8	60	.32	.43	.60	.65	.76	.74	.58	.61
9-11	59	.50	.66	.70	.78	.85	.73	.67	.65
12-14	46	.23	.38	.41	.49	.71	.63	.44	.43
15-17	30	.22	.37	.34	.44	.68	.67	.41	.45
Females by age									
3-5	11	.53	.68	.69	.56	.72	.71	.74	.67
6-8	42	.28	.37	.28	.38	.47	.64	.36	.45
9-11	49	.28	.49	.38	.51	.49	.53	.38	.48
12-14	48	.15	.23	.19	.27	.32	.42	.18	.24
15-17	25	.33	.68	.32	.63	.45	.47	.36	.62

Note. Norms are taken from "Normative Data on Revised Conners Parent and Teacher Rating Scales" by C. H. Goyette, C. K. Conners, and R. F. Ulrich, 1978, *Journal of Abnormal Child Psychology, 6,* p. 233. Copyright 1978 by Plenum Publishing Corp. Reprinted by permission. The scores are derived by assigning 0, 1, 2, or 3 points to the answers of "not at all," "just a little," "pretty much," and "very much," respectively, for each item. The points for each item assigned to each factor are then summed and divided by the number of items in that factor or category to get the factor score. The items assigned to each factor or category from the original Conners Teacher's Rating Scale are as follows: Conduct Problems: questions 4, 5, 6, 10, 11, 12, 23, and 27; Hyperactivity: questions 1, 2, 3, 8, 14, 15, and 16; Inattention-Passivity: questions 7, 9, 18, 20, 21, 22, 26, and 28; Hyperactivity index; questions 1, 5, 7, 8, 10, 11, 14, 15, 21, and 26.
$^a n$ = number of subjects per age group.

teractions. We have employed a modified form of this coding system for use in our own clinic and employ different playroom situations than those used by Forehand and McMahon to assess parent–child interactions (i.e., Child's Game and Parent's Game). The recording form and instructions for its use are provided in Part 3 of this manual. Recording occurs in 1-minute blocks, listed along the left-hand side of the coding matrix. Within each minute, the observer circles the behaviors of interest that occur. Parent and child behaviors are marked using numbered columns. Each column is used when the parent gives a new command or task to the child. When the parent issues a new command, C is circled. Each time the parent repeats this

Table 2.5. Norms for the School Situations Questionnaire

Age (years)	n	Number of problem settings	Mean severity
Boys			
6-8	170	2.4 (3.3)	1.5 (2.0)
9-11	123	2.8 (3.2)	1.9 (2.1)
Girls			
6-8	180	1.0 (2.0)	0.8 (1.5)
9-11	126	1.3 (2.1)	0.8 (1.2)

Note. Table entries are means with standard deviations in parentheses. Reprinted with permission from Michael J. Breen, Ph.D.

command, R is circled. The initials Cpy are circled below the word "Child" if the child complies with the initial command within 10 seconds. Otherwise, the initials Ncpy are circled, indicating noncompliance to the initial command. The 10-second interval for the child to comply begins when the initial command (C) is given. Compliance to the repeat commands (R) is not scored. If the child displays opposition, refusal, whining, complaining, or behavior resistant to the initial or any repeated command, then the negative behavior category is scored (Neg). If the parent attends to or praises the child's compliance to this command, A is circled below the column marked "Par."; and if the the parent yells at, reprimands, or behaves negatively toward the child, then PNeg is circled. With the exception of repeat commands (R), all other categories are scored only once during those parent–child interactions surrounding a command.

In short, the observer records what the parent does, what the child does in response to the parent's commands, and the parent's reaction to the child's behavior. All of these parent and child behaviors would be scored within column 1 until the parent issued a new command to the child. At that time, the observer would move to column 2 and begin scoring parent and child behavior again. That is, the new command would be scored by circling C, and anytime it is repeated, R is circled. The child would be scored as complying (Cpy) to this initial command if compliance began within 10 seconds of the initial command. Other categories are scored as described above. There is sufficient room in each row for five new commands to be given within each minute of observation. The observer continues recording along row 1 of the matrix for minute 1 until the next minute occurs, at which time the coder moves down to row 2 and begins scoring parent and child behavior again. There is room for up to 10 minutes of recording on one sheet. For observation periods beyond 10 minutes, a second coding sheet is used.

These observations are taken in a clinic playroom that has a one-way mirror and intercom. The room contains a sofa, coffee table, armchair, several small worktables, an adult's desk chair, and a child's desk chair. Toys are set out on one of the worktables for play purposes. Magazines are provided on the coffee table. The parent and child are taken into this playroom and told to play as they might do at home. This interval lasts for 5 minutes and serves as an habituation period to the playroom. No formal coding of interactions is done within this period, but the examiner may wish to take informal notes of any clinically significant interaction problems witnessed in this interval. After the habituation period, the examiner enters the room and provides the parent with a list of 10 tasks to do with the child. These are set forth in Table 2.6. These instructions for the parent are typed on a separate sheet of paper and provided to him or her at the beginning of the task situation. Behavior in this situation is recorded by the observer for 10 minutes. This coding system significantly discriminates clinic-referred from normal children and is sensitive to drug and parent training program interventions.

You may wish to design other tasks to use in this situation. The essential element is that the parent be provided with a list of age-appropriate tasks to have a child accomplish. For those not having a playroom with observation mirror, these behaviors can be coded during a visit to the family's home. If this is done, then the observer instructs the parent and child to remain within one room, usually the living room or family room, and the coder occupies a chair off to the side of the room, remaining as unobtrusive as possible. After a brief period of time to allow the child to habituate to the presence of the coder, the child is then asked by the parent to perform a list of commands previously given to the parent by the observer.

Where observing in the home is not feasible, the clinician can request the parent to maintain a diary of a particular noncompliant behavior over the course of the next week. The parent and clinician agree on the specific behavior to be recorded. Usually a situation from the Home Situations Questionnaire can be used (e.g., getting dressed or doing homework). The parent can be asked to record the

Table 2.6. Two Sets of Tasks for Use in Clinic Playroom Observations of Parent–Child Interactions of Noncompliant Children

Set 1	*Set 2*
1. Stand up please	1. Come here and let me fix your shirt/blouse
2. Open the door	
3. Give me one of those toys	2. Put these toys away in their boxes
4. Put all of the toys in their boxes	3. Empty that wastebasket into the other one near the door
5. Put the toys and their boxes on the shelves	
6. Put the chairs under the tables	4. Fold these clothes neatly and put them in the box (old child-size clothes are provided)
7. Take off your shoes	
8. Sit at the table and draw copies of these three designs (geometric designs are given)	5. Put these metal pegs in the holes in this box (child is given the Grooved Pegboard Test)
9. Do this sheet of math problems (math problems are given)	6. Walk this black line on the floor slowly heel to toe (black tape line is on floor)
10. Put your shoes on	7. Stack the magazines neatly on the table
	8. Put the toys back on the table
	9. Wipe off the table with this cloth
	10. Pick up these papers on the floor

date and time, the command requested of the child, a frequency count of the number of times it was repeated (usually using hash marks in the diary), and how the parent resolved the situation.

All of these methods of recording parent–child interactions can be used during the initial evaluation and repeated during and after the parent training course to assess the degree of change in parent–child interactions achieved by the program. Some clinicians may wish to assess the degree of parent satisfaction with the parent training program once it is completed. If so, I recommend the Parent's Consumer Satisfaction Questionnaire in the text by Forehand and McMahon (1981).

SCREENING FAMILIES FOR PARENT TRAINING

No single treatment program is successful for all clients. Recognizing this, researchers have recently studied those factors that predict success or failure within a parent training program such as this. It should be obvious that conditions that affect the parents undergoing training will have some affect on their success in this program. For instance, parental psychiatric problems can interfere with that parent's ability to acquire and utilize the information in the training program, if not attendance at the meetings themselves. Parents who are actively psychotic or drug dependent during training will have a difficult time consistently utilizing the procedures with a behavior problem child, assuming they can follow them at all. Similarly, chronic health problems that affect their behavior may interfere to some degree with effective child management. While there is little research on this issue, my clinical experience suggests that certain chronic medical conditions such as migraine headaches, epilepsy, premenstrual tension syndrome, and diabetes impair the implementation of the child management procedures. Several parental characteristics that have been repeatedly shown to predict poor outcome in training are maternal depression, marital discord, maternal isolation (insularity) from the social community, and family socioeconomic status (Dumas & Wahler, 1983; Firestone & Witt, 1982; Forehand & McMahon, 1981; Strain, Young, & Horowitz, 1981). These variables relate to outcome in a linear way so that the greater their degree or severity within a family, the poorer the prognosis in training. Exercising careful judgment, the clinician must, when these factors are present, decide whether or not they should be addressed (where possible) before beginning training.

In a similar way, certain conditions affecting the child may impede the successful implementation of child management programs. Obviously, the type and severity of the child's behavior problems should be considered in the decision to undertake this or similar training regimens. Physical aggression and assault by the child may be sufficiently likely that residential treatment would be a more prudent alternative to parent training, at least initially. Once the child's coercive behaviors have been brought under control within a more closely supervised environment, parent training could then serve as a therapy program for the transition of the child back into the home and the preparation of the parents for such a successful transition. Children with severe language delays or significant mental delays may not respond as well to this program because of its emphasis on compliance to verbal commands and rules. In my experience, children having a mental or language age of at least two years can respond successfully to these procedures. Greater time may be needed in working with the parents of such a child, particularly with practice sessions in the clinic, but improvement in child behavior in such cases is certainly possible.

FEASIBILITY OF HOMEWORK ASSIGNMENTS AND TRAINING METHODS

Because the present program contains a variety of homework assignments to be done by parents, you must consider how feasible such assignments are for a given family and whether they should be modified to fit the individual characteristics of the parent or child. Less educated or intelligent parents may require less reading material but greater modeling and explanation of the procedures to successfully understand them. Parents with sensory handicaps may need special devices for recording their assignments, as in using a tape recorder for recording the homework situations where a parent is partially blind or is illiterate.

How the methods are taught may also be slightly modified to fit the unique aspects of your clinical situation or the family in training. A few parents may even need or wish to record the training sessions in order to review them between sessions. Both research (Webster-Stratton, 1984) and clinical experience suggest that in some instances videotaped instruction or examples of child management procedures can also be effective in parent training programs and are more cost-effective than individual training of families. In general, you need to be sensitive to the individual and unique characteristics of each family and adjust the homework and training methods accordingly.

In so doing, you must decide whether individual or group parent training is to be used. Training individual families in these procedures is certainly effective, especially when augmented with live demonstrations of the methods and the opportunity for parents to practice these procedures with their child under the supervision of the therapist. Using a "bug in the ear" transmitting device combined with a clinic playroom, one-way mirror, and adjacent observation room can greatly enhance the ability immediately to direct, shape, and reinforce parent management of children (Eyberg & Matarazzo, 1980).

However, the heavy caseloads of many clinicians do not always permit the training of individual families in all instances. As a result, group training may be necessary where four to eight sets of parents attend classes without their children. Group training has the advantage of allowing parents to commiserate about their experiences with the behavior problem children as well as to share possible solutions each has found in dealing with certain problems. Parents also develop a sense of camaraderie with others in the group, which, in many cases, increases their motivation to carry out the homework assignments, particularly when they must describe their success at implementing the methods at the next group meeting. Studies comparing group versus individual training (Christensen, Johnson, Phillips, & Glasgow, 1980) have found group training to be as effective as individual training, while substantially reducing professional time involved in training. Yet some parents may be easily intimidated by the more outspoken or successful couples in a group or require more individualized instruction in order to properly grasp the methods. Clinical experience with the program shows that not all families respond well to group training, and so some screening criteria for assigning parents to individual or group treatment should be exercised by the therapist. Generally, parents with more severely disturbed children, those of low educational or economic attainment, or those with multiple risk factors in the family (described above) should be assigned at least initially to individualized training programs.

SUMMARY

This chapter has reviewed several approaches to the assessment of noncompliance in clinic-referred children. An approach is recommended that incorporates a highly specific interview on parent–child interactions, the use of rating scales to assess child deviance, and direct observations of parent–child interactions during task performance. These measures can be taken both prior to and after completion of the parent training program to evaluate improvements in parent–child relations. The assessment will also reveal several characteristics of the parents and children that are associated with poor outcome in training and should be considered for screening parents out of this child management training program. Other parent characteristics will have some bearing on how the homework assignments are individualized to a family's circumstances.

CHAPTER THREE

Practical Implemention of This Program

LOGISTICAL AND PRACTICAL CONSIDERATIONS IN TRAINING

Upon first learning this program, clinicians often ask several questions of practical import, such as whether it is necessary for both parents to attend the training sessions, if the sessions should be conducted in the clinic or the home, and how they should handle parents who fail to comply with the homework assignments. The answers to such questions clearly depend upon many of the characteristics of a given family. However, some general advice can be offered.

While I have found it useful for both parents to attend the training sessions where possible, and appointments are provided late in the afternoon or early evening at times to accommodate working parents, research suggests it is not imperative for both parents to attend in order for successful intervention to occur (Adesso & Lipson, 1981; Firestone, Kelly, & Fike, 1980; Martin, 1977). What appears to be important is whether the absent parent, usually the father, is supportive of the attendance of the spouse and the implementation of the practices in the home. For now, it seems best to encourage fathers to attend the parent training sessions, but treatment should not be denied to a parent merely because a spouse cannot attend.

In the case of single parents, this is not an issue. However, you may find that the single parent reports greater distress over the child's misbehavior, perhaps due to being unable to share such a burden with a supportive spouse. Supervision or training of the child may be impossible in the afternoon hours on weekdays should this parent also work outside the home, leaving the care of the child to sitters less skilled in child management tactics. Hence, success of the program may be somewhat diminished in some of these cases. Nevertheless, many single parents can and often do succeed in acquiring and effectively using the skills of this program with a behavior disordered child.

Few studies have examined the issue of whether training in the clinic is as effective as that done in the family's home. What little research exists suggests that in-home training does not appreciably increase the effectiveness of parent training programs (Worland, Carney, Milich, & Grame, 1980), while it certainly increases the cost of the services. In some states, insurance companies may not reimburse for such out-of-office services, making the issue moot for those clinicians who derive their livelihood from such sources of compensation. My experience suggests that training in the clinic setting can be quite successful, less time consuming, less costly, and as effective as in-home training for most families. It has been my impression that going into the family's home so artificially alters that environment that it differs little from the artificial surroundings of the clinic playroom in terms of enhancing treatment. While an appreciation for the physical layout of the home and its condition can aid somewhat in individualizing certain management methods to that particular family, it is often outweighed by the additional time and expense involved in going to the home.

Your management of parental noncompliance with the treatment methods is not so easily addressed. When parents return to the next session of training without doing homework, how should you handle the matter? In the training of more than 3,000 clinicians in this program over the past 10 years, the following methods have been offered and found useful. First, it should be clear that training in additional methods should not occur until the issue of noncompliance and its causes are addressed. In other words, parents are not permitted to advance to the next step in the program until they have mastered the step under discussion to the satisfaction of the clinician. Thus, it may take some families several weeks longer than others to advance through the steps of the program. For families in a group training program, one missed homework assignment is permitted. This family must meet with the therapist for an individual appointment to make up the missed appointment or homework assignment before the next group meeting. Families that miss more than one group meeting or homework assignment are discontinued from the group and offered individual training if they so desire.

Second, you should address immediately the reasons for failing to carry out the assignments. Often, legitimate reasons exist. In these instances, the session is a brief one, and parents are requested to try the assignment again in the coming week. Where little apparent reason exists for the parental noncompliance, you may have to inquire skillfully about parental motivation for training or family stress events that may be interfering with training (such as marital discord, alcohol abuse, or financial hardships). In some cases, training may be temporarily discontinued while the family stress event is managed or the parent is referred to another professional for intervention aimed at the stressor.

A third method for coping with parental noncompliance is to establish a "breakage" fee (Patterson, 1982) whereby parents leave a fixed sum of money with the therapist and a portion of this is mailed to the parents' most-hated political or other organization for each missed assignment. Having the therapist keep the money may not be as successful, since some parents feel that the therapist may deserve it for having been inconvenienced. This money is not part of the fee for therapy but is specifically identified for this purpose of motivating compliance. It is also possible to return a portion of the money to the parents for each assignment done correctly as a method of reinforcing parental compliance with the program. Some therapists may choose to implement both procedures with a given family.

In some cases where chronic parental noncompliance has occurred, this should be well documented and therapy discontinued. The parents may be told that should they change their minds and decide to cooperate with training they may return.

CLINICAL AND STYLISTIC CONSIDERATIONS

It is well known that treatment efforts can succeed or fail merely on the basis of the manner or style in which they are presented to a family. A large part of treatment efficacy can be traced to "placebo" or nonspecific factors associated with clinicians, their characteristics and manner of interacting with others, and the confidence and enthusiasm they project in their methods as they teach them. The specific treatment procedures, while obviously important, are of little effectiveness if clinicians cannot convincingly persuade parents of the importance of the procedures and their efficacy. These remarks and those that follow may seem obvious to skilled clinicians, but they are rarely stated in scientific papers on these treatment programs and may be overlooked even by the experienced clinician. Granted, there are varying preferences among clinicians on these issues of style. The points presented here are obviously ones that I favor and have found to work well in previous treatment cases. You should therefore view them as the suggestions they are, rather than as an inflexible set of rules to be applied equally to all cases.

I have found a general Socratic style of conveying concepts and behavioral principles to parents to be most helpful. This seems to help parents consider themselves an important part of the process of engineering programs for their children instead of fools or simpletons who must receive direct lecturing. Clinicians using such a style question the parents and lead them to the correct conclusion, concept, or method in such a manner that the parents feel that they have either achieved the solution on their own or at least contributed to its discovery. It is felt that this method leaves a more lasting impression of the material with the parents and perhaps helps to maintain their motivation in treatment. Moreover, it avoids the implication present in any directive style of teaching, that the parents are completely ignorant of child management principles—a myth that will be quickly dispelled by only a few cases of parent training. While parents may not be able to use professional terminology to describe these principles, they are often accurate in describing the actual processes involved. Certainly, there will be times where a more directive style is necessary, particularly in describing and modeling a specific method or in outlining the homework assignment for a particular step of the program. When pressed for time, you may elect to engage in direct lecturing in order to cover large amounts of material, but in my experience this is generally detrimental to parents' long-term acquisition of that material.

A corollary of this Socratic style is that professional jargon is to be avoided where possible. Efforts to teach parents the terminology of behavioral psychology hardly guarantee that they have understood the underlying principles sufficiently to insure their use of them outside of therapy. Employing such jargon as "contingencies of reinforcement," "extinction," and "stimulus control" is overly pedantic and self-aggrandizing and unnecessarily restricts the educational or intellectual range of parents to whom these methods can be taught. Use of jargon is also likely to be viewed as dry, boring, or unintelligible by most parents who lack some college education, and this certainly affects the compliance of these parents to therapy. There is also no empirical evidence to show that using such jargon enhances treatment efficacy. In the absence of these data, I feel that behavioral jargon is more of a hindrance than a help to teaching effective child management. It is left to you to decide whether, as a parent, you would prefer to hear that you should "periodically praise a child for complying with requests" or should "provide social secondary reinforcers on an intermittent schedule contingent upon the occurrence of compliant responses to verbal demands."

A Socratic method of teaching parents also seems to avoid a problem that is probably quite common in therapy—parental dependence on the therapist. When you alone design behavioral programs and then hand them to parents for use, the parents may fail to gain the problem-solving skills needed for dealing with present and future child behavior problems. Week after week, such parents come to therapy to lay additional problems at the feet of the "great behavioral engineer" (you!), without ever understanding the basic principles used by you to design these programs. Such dependence will be hard to discontinue as treatment termination nears. While this problem has not been widely studied, many clinicians would agree that parents who understand the principles and concepts that serve as the basis for a management method are more likely to use it than those who have been shown only the method.

Many behavioral therapists have noted that the principles that they are attempting to convey to parents for use with their children are quite similar to those that they use in training the parents themselves. This obviously means that ample praise and appreciation are shown to parents upon their participation in therapeutic discussions, accomplishment of behavioral record-keeping, and implementation of suggested treatment methods. Disapproval and withdrawal of reinforcers (such as breakage fees), as noted earlier, are often contingent on parental noncompliance to the suggested methods.

During each session, it is imperative that you periodically stop the discussion of new material and assess the parents' understanding of what has been presented. In addition, you should invite the parents' opinions as to how the method under discussion will fit into their particular schedule or style and how it may be used with their children in particular. This often reveals factors that would have hampered or precluded compliance to the method and suggests that it may have to be modified to form a "best fit" with a particular family. The greater the discrepancy between the treatment demands and family life-styles, the less compliance to treatment there will be. While this may be obvious to the sophisticated reader, it is often overlooked in clinic situations when time is at a premium and caseloads are large.

A similar caution applies to leaping into new material at the beginning of a therapy session without first reviewing what has transpired in the life of a family since the last session or determining how well the homework assignment has succeeded. Overlooking such obvious stylistic precautions will often result in the errors being forcefully brought to your attention later in the session via a variety of client reactions. One may be apparent boredom or inattention to what clinicians are saying because of preoccupation with the as yet unacknowledged problem. Other clients may more assertively interrupt to present the complication, for example that a spouse has deserted the home, a serious medical problem has arisen for a family member, or the method assigned for homework has resulted in serious misfortune for a parent or child. Such revelations often dictate that the course of therapy be altered or temporarily postponed until these new issues are addressed.

In discussing the behavioral methods, you should take care to invite the parents to modify or embellish the methods to meet specific needs in their family situation. Here it may be your turn to learn a new thing or two from the clearly greater experience parents have with their particular children. This is nicely illustrated by a case in which parents were being taught to use a time out procedure in public settings, such as stores, where a chair or corner was not available for isolating the child contingent on misbehavior. I explained that using a small pocket notebook to record the child's misbehavior and making the child aware of this beforehand might help. For every entry in the book, the child would have to spend 10 minutes in a time out chair upon returning home. In the next session, the parents explained that they had tried this method but added a quite novel twist to it. They had taken a Polaroid picture of the child seated in his time out chair at home and placed this in the spiral pocket notebook they were taking to the store. Before entering the store, they handed him the picture and reminded him that this was where he would wind up at home if misbehavior occurred. I have found this embellishment to be of such practical value that it is now described to each new set of parents we train as part of the handout for the session on public misbehavior.

As noted earlier, parents are rarely ignorant of effective behavioral methods or principles and can serve as satisfactory "cotherapists" at some points in therapy. I have found it useful to explain at the beginning of therapy the need for such collaboration. This serves a secondary function of letting parents know that clinicians do not necessarily have all of the answers to their children's problems. While you may be an expert about general behavioral principles and technology, the parents are the obvious experts about their particular children, their habits, their temperaments, and their reaction patterns. Acting as if parents know nothing about child behavior principles is both patronizing and professionally naive. Without the integration of information from both sets of "experts," therapy is much less likely to succeed.

It almost goes without saying that interspersed throughout therapy should be periodic expressions of empathy for parents' or families' current circumstances, and especially for the work needed to use this program well. Acknowledgments that the methods being discussed are easy to read but not so easy to put into effect are helpful. Reminders about the importance of doing homework regularly and practicing the methods should also be periodically given. Often it can be helpful to draw analogies between learning child management skills and acquiring new skills with musical instruments or recreational sports. Parents are usually quick to give therapists total credit for any success at improving their children's behavior. It should be made obvious to them that the success is partly if not solely due to their use of the behavioral method, since no tool left on the shelf miraculously fixes a problem.

SCHEDULING SESSIONS

While parent training sessions may be scheduled throughout your typical clinic day, I have found it useful to set aside late afternoon times for this program so as to encourage parents to attend without jeopardizing their employment. Training of individual families is done through weekly visits typically lasting 1 hour. Parent training groups may also be organized, in which case weekly meetings last 2 to 2.5 hours and no more than six to eight families are included. As noted earlier, the decision to place a family in group versus individual therapy often revolves around issues of parental educational level, type, number, and severity of the child's problems, degree of family stress, and the extent of individual attention a family may require.

SUMMARY

This chapter has reviewed various practical issues involved in the clinical implementation of the program, such as coping with parental noncompliance, considering style in training, and scheduling therapy sessions. A sensible, pragmatic, and unpretentious approach makes clear to parents the demands of the program and the specific methods to use, while the clinician remains empathic and solicitous of parental participation.

CHAPTER FOUR

Overview of
the Training Program

Before reviewing in detail the specific methods to be taught in each step of the program, it is necessary to examine the basic concepts upon which the training program is built, the rationale for the sequence of the steps, and the schedule of activities occurring within each session.

CONCEPTS UNDERLYING CHILD MANAGEMENT TRAINING

Several important principles of child management are interwoven throughout the training sequence. To grasp fully the program's orientation and potential power, practitioners should know these concepts in advance.

1. Immediacy of consequences. Consequences for child behavior, be they positive or negative, must be provided as immediately as possible if parents are to gain effective control over inappropriate behavior. You should repeatedly stress that parents need to provide consequences for a child immediately after the occurrence of the behavior of interest rather than waiting several minutes or hours to confront the problem or reward the appropriate behavior. Because of the hectic life-styles of many families, most parents delay dealing with behaviors, especially positive or appropriate ones. They are often much quicker to attend to undesirable or especially intrusive behaviors. But, even with these, they often wait until after the fourth or fifth repetition of a command before confronting their children's noncompliance. In short, the more immediately parents can provide consequences to a child, the greater the control they will exert over that child's behavior.

2. *Specificity of consequences.* Parents are also instructed that consequences, especially verbal or social ones, should be quite specific. Both praise and criticism should refer to the behavior at issue, instead of being vague, general, or nebulous references to the children themselves, their general behavior, or their personal integrity. Similarly, punishment should be tailored to fit the transgression and not based upon the parents' level of impatience or frustration over this or prior episodes of misbehavior.

3. *Consistency of consequences.* Virtually all behavioral approaches to parent training stress the concept of consistency of consequences as a key to greater control of child behavior. This refers to consistency across settings, over time, and between parents. Consistency across settings simply means that if a behavior occurs that is generally punished in one environment, say the home, then it is also punished in other environments, such as stores. While there may be occasional exceptions to this rule, it is generally a good policy for parents to respond to child behaviors similarly across various social contexts. This is often contrary to the practice of many parents who handle a problem one way when at home and a different way when in public places where others may observe them. Such a practice directly trains the child as to which situation will prove successful for the display of misbehavior.

Consistency over time simply means that parental standards about acceptable and unacceptable behavior in children should not vary too greatly from one moment to the next. Although these standards will change as a function of developmental changes in the child, over more immediate time periods it is necessary for parents to provide consequences for behavior as consistently as possible. Child behavior that is defined as unacceptable on one day should not be arbitrarily tolerated or even reinforced on another. For instance, punishing a child for raiding the refrigerator when a parent has a headache, while ignoring or actually assisting a visit to the refrigerator at a future time is a ludicrous practice that greatly reinforces such rule violations in the home. The converse is also true: a behavior that is rewarded today should be so in the future and should certainly not be subjected to punishment later.

Consistency between parents in the rules they establish for children and the consequences they employ for their adherence or violation is also important. Quite frequently, mothers tend to manage the problems they experience with a child in ways very different from those of the fathers; this often leads to conflicts not only in the development of a consistent set of rules for the children but also in the marital relationship.

4. *Establishment of incentive programs before punishment.* Another concept is that punishment for inappropriate behavior should not be introduced in the home unless the parents have established a specific program for rewarding the appropriate alternative behavior. Most parents phrase their concerns about child behavior in the negative, specifying what it is they dislike about a child. This naturally leads to a consideration of punishment methods to suppress the unwanted behavior. As a result, punishment is the major type of interaction in the family, and children rarely receive reinforcement for whatever acceptable behavior may be shown. Furthermore, punishment appears to lose its effectiveness in circumstances where the family environment is devoid of positive incentives for appropriate conduct. If parents are taught to rephrase their complaints about child behavior into prosocial or appropriate alternatives, the natural response is one of thinking of incentives to encourage an increase in this behavior. Only then should consideration be given to punishment methods for reducing the unacceptable behavior by the child. This is especially true in those sessions where punishment is being taught, lest parents perceive the therapist as advocating the use of punishment as a primary response to misconduct by children.

5. *Anticipation of and planning for misbehavior.* The experienced clinician recognizes that many parents are as impulsive in their reactions to child misbehavior as their children are in reacting to their own problems. This results in parents spending tremendous amounts of time in managing misbehavior while investing minimal, if any, time in analyzing and anticipating those situations in which the children are likely to create problems. If parents were to anticipate problematic encounters, they might develop methods that

would tend to reduce the probability of those problems developing. Perhaps this apparent lack of forethought or anticipation is merely the result of being so overwhelmed with incorrigible behavior that it is difficult to "take the offensive" and try to anticipate and ward off future problems in a particular setting. Or perhaps it in fact contributes to some of the difficulties parents have in dealing with children in particular places such as stores and restaurants. In any event, it is necessary to periodically discuss this issue of thinking ahead about problem situations and preparing a plan of behavior management for the child before entering the potential problem situation. This is certainly contrary to the more typical situation of waiting until the disruptive or unmanageable behavior occurs and then trying to determine what to do about it.

6. *Reciprocity of family interactions.* Another concept conveyed to parents throughout the program is that of reciprocity of interactions within families. Parents often have a unilateral view of the causes of child behavior problems—either they caused the problem or it is all the child's fault. You must periodically emphasize that interaction patterns within families are quite complex and not especially well understood at this time. What *is* known strongly indicates that parents' behavior toward a child is partly a function of that child's behavior toward them, the child's temperament, physical characteristics and abilities, and prior experiences with that child. Similarly, the child's behavior is partly a function of how the parent treats the child, the parents' own temperament, physical characteristics and abilities, and prior experiences with that parent. Because of this bidirectional influence between parent and child, it is difficult to assign blame to either party for the current state of conflict. Hence, this program does not waste time blaming parents *or* children for interaction problems. Instead, all parties to the problematic interaction bear some responsibility for its resolution. That parents are chosen as the major focus of change has more to do with convenience and their motivation to alter the problem interactions than it does with finding fault with their child management skills.

In summary, several general concepts concerning child management deserve periodic emphasis throughout the course of therapy: (1) immediacy and (2) specificity of consequences; (3) consistency of consequences across settings, over time, and between parents; (4) establishment of incentive programs for appropriate behavior before implementation of punishment methods to suppress its unacceptable alternative; (5) anticipation of potential problem situations and preparation of a plan of action; and (6) reciprocity of interaction patterns in families and uselessness of fault-finding.

SEQUENCE OF STEPS WITHIN THE PROGRAM

There are 10 steps to the core parent training program. These can be taught as one self-contained unit with therapy terminating after the final session, or they can be integrated into an ongoing family therapy or parent counseling program designed to address other difficulties in the family, marriage, or parent's personal life. In some cases, it may be necessary to change to other forms of therapy after these steps are completed in order to address other problems of the child, such as enuresis or encopresis. In any case, the sequence of the procedures within this core program should remain essentially the same. Much research and clinical experience have been invested in constructing the steps of the program and their sequence, and they are deliberately presented in this order for significant reasons. Although it is possible that some families may not require all steps of the program because of the mild nature of the child's noncompliance, the training chosen for any particular case should follow this order. The justification is that the initial sessions emphasize the development of positive behavior management methods within the family, especially the use of incentives for compliance with rules and commands, while later sessions deal specifically with punishment techniques. Inverting the sequence so that punishment is taught first usually results in an excessive reliance by parents on punishment throughout the entire program as well as a lessened effectiveness of such techniques. After a home environment rich with incentives for appropriate behavior is established, the introduction of punishment appears to go more smoothly and effectively.

In cases of only minor noncompliance by a child, a therapist may choose to train the parents only in the use of praise for acceptable compliance and appropriate child behavior and then skip to the use of the time out procedure for the occasional noncompliance by the child. In such instances, parents will generally find these two procedures to be sufficiently effective without the need for the more intense contingency management procedures and discussions of the causes of child misbehavior. Here, even the time out procedure need not be as dramatic or intense as it is in the usual approach, since the minor level of noncompliance does not warrant such theatrics. Occasionally, the therapist may implement the home poker chip or point systems to augment the enhanced use of praise with these children, often with great success. Nonetheless, even in such mild cases, the sequence remains the same—positive reinforcement and incentive methods are taught before the punishment procedures are introduced.

In most cases, the complete sequence of steps should be taught.

Step 1: Why Children Misbehave. This session is intended to teach parents the typical causes of child misbehavior, how they interact, and what parents can do to begin identifying such causes within their own children and family.

Step 2: Pay Attention! The value of parental attention to the child is quite low at the beginning of therapy, making it almost useless in many cases as a way of motivating better child behavior. This session is intended to train parents in ways of eliminating ineffective or even detrimental attending while increasing more effective forms of attending to and appreciating child behavior.

Step 3: Increasing Compliance to Commands and Requests. After more valuable and effective attending skills have been developed in parents, the skills are directed specifically at improving child compliance by contingently responding to it with acknowledgment, appreciation, and praise.

Step 4: Decreasing Disruptiveness—Increasing Independent Play. An extension of Step 3, this step provides parents with instruction in how to attend to children when they are not interrupting or bothering their parents at times when parents may be engaged in an activity (e.g., talking on the telephone, working in the kitchen, or speaking to a visitor). By interrupting their own activities frequently to positively attend to a child's independent play, parents are able to increase those periods that children are not bothersome during parental activities.

Step 5: When Praise Is Not Enough—Poker Chips and Points. Recognizing that praise and attention are rarely sufficient by themselves to motivate better compliance in clinic-referred children, the therapist requires the parents to implement a highly effective motivational program that enlists a variety of rewards and incentives readily available within the home to increase child compliance with commands, rules, chores, and codes of social conduct in the home.

This program is quite useful for children of mental ages of 4 years and older. Poker chips are used as tokens for 4- to 8-year-olds while 9- to 11-year-olds are provided with points recorded in a notebook. Children earn points or chips, contingent on acceptable compliance to rules and commands, and may use these tokens for the purchase of daily, weekly, or long-term privileges and rewards.

Step 6: Time Out! In this step, parents receive instruction in how to use the token system described above as a form of punishment, or response cost (i.e., penalties in the token program are assessed for inappropriate behavior). However, much of this step is devoted to a detailed discussion of a procedure known as time out from reinforcement, or simply time out. This procedure involves immediately isolating the child to a chair in a dull corner of the home, contingent on the occurrence of noncompliance or unacceptable social conduct. Parents may use this time out method for only one or two misbehaviors, utilizing fines within the token system for managing other types of misconduct.

Step 7: Extending Time Out to Other Misbehaviors. Once parents are effectively employing the time out technique, they are permitted to expand its use to an additional one or two misbehaviors by the children. Where problems have been encountered in using the method, much of this session is devoted to troubleshooting the problems with implemention of time out and correcting them.

Step 8: Managing Noncompliance in Public Places. Up to this point, parents have been instructed to use the treatment procedures only within the home. At this step, parents are trained to use slightly modified versions of the techniques for managing child misbehavior in public places, such as stores, restaurants, and church. The training incorporates a method known as "think aloud—think ahead," wherein parents establish a plan for managing misconduct immediately before entering any public building, share the plan with the children, and adhere to their plan while in the public place.

Step 9: Handling Future Behavior Problems. Parents are briefly instructed in how these procedures might be used for other behavior problems that the child does not now have. In addition, parents are quizzed as to how they might design a behavior-change program based upon the methods they have been using.

Step 10: Booster Sessions. Parents are requested to return for a 1-month booster session to assess their adherence to the treatment methods, plan on the fading out of the home token system should that be appropriate, and help troubleshoot any problems they may now be encountering. Parents are cautioned about slippage or regression in their management tactics—the return to previously ineffective and punishment-dominated methods—and are encouraged to remain with the treatment techniques for as long as possible. They are then scheduled to be seen in 3 months for a follow-up visit in which progress and problems are reassessed (and re-treated if necessary).

SEQUENCE OF ACTIVITIES WITHIN EACH SESSION

After the first step, the sessions follow a standard pattern of events. Each session begins with a review of the previous week's homework assignment and any other events the family may wish to share with you. Problems that may have arisen in implementing prior instructions are discussed and resolved. As already noted, should parents fail to have done the homework, this issue is addressed and the parents are reassigned this homework for the next week. When this occurs, no new material would be discussed in the session. If homework was done satisfactorily, the new material, concepts, and methods are introduced. Where appropriate, you should model or demonstrate these methods. Some may choose to use videotaped demonstrations of the techniques to enhance the parents' acquisition of the method.

At this point, practice of the methods within the sessions is encouraged. In the case where a family is treated individually, the parent and child would go to a playroom, and the parent would practice the methods with the child under your supervision through a one-way mirror, if available. Any of several "bug in the ear"[1] transmitter devices may be used, through which the parent, using a small hearing aid that receives transmissions from an adjoining observation room, is given direct and immediate feedback during practice. Should this resource not be available, simply observing the parents and child in a portion of your office for 15 minutes and then discussing with the parent the impressions from the performance can serve the same purpose. Where a parent group is being used for training, it is possible to pair up the parents and have each dyad adjourn to separate corners of the conference room or classroom; one

1. This piece of equipment may be obtained from the Farrell Instrument Co.

parent pretends to be a child while the other role-plays the method under discussion. You can move from one dyad to the next, giving feedback on the performance of the "parent." Then the parents reverse roles, and practice continues. Again, you should spend a brief period of time with each dyad, providing feedback to the adult in the parent role.

You would then discuss any problems the parents might envision in implementing the technique in their home the coming week. Subsequently, the homework for the coming week is assigned, and questions regarding it are resolved. You should provide throughout each session ample praise, encouragement, and positive feedback for the parents' compliance to the instructions and homework.

SUMMARY

This chapter has described the important concepts or principles upon which the treatment methods are founded, as well as the 10 steps of the program and their sequence. Emphasis is placed on adhering to the particular pattern of training as important in its own right, not simply in the methods being taught. Which methods are introduced in what sequence is often crucial to enhancing the effectiveness of the total program. A method for organizing the material to be taught within each step is also presented.

2

Guidelines for Therapists in Conducting Each Step of the Program

This section provides detailed guidelines for conducting each of the steps of the parent training program. Within each step, goals of that step are specifically stated, an outline for use in the session is provided, and specific instructions for conducting that step are described. You will want to review the sequence of activities within each session as described in chapter 4 of Part 1 before beginning treatment with each new case. You will also find it helpful to refer to the outline provided for each step while conducting that step of the program so as to insure that all of the important information is reviewed with the parents. Finally, the parent handouts which accompany each step are set forth in Part 3. Defiant Children: Parent–Teacher Assignments, *the workbook which goes along with this manual, was designed for sharing with each family seen in therapy. Additional sets should be purchased separately from The Guilford Press.*

Why Children Misbehave

GOALS

1. To educate parents concerning the causes of childhood misbehavior.
2. To urge parents to identify those causes or contributors to misbehavior that may exist in their families.
3. To encourage parents to begin to remedy those causes of misbehavior that can be rectified within their families.

MATERIALS REQUIRED

- Parent handouts
    Profile of Child and Parent Characteristics
    Family Problems Inventory
- Diagram of noncompliant interaction (Figure 1.1)

STEP OUTLINE

- Review of events since the evaluation
- Open discussion of parents' views of the causes of misbehavior
- Presentation of a model for understanding child misbehavior
    Child's characteristics
    Parents' characteristics
    Situational consequences
    Family stress events
    Reciprocal interaction among these factors

- Goal of therapy: Designing a "best fit" between parent, child, and the family circumstances
- Some handicaps are behavioral: The need for a prosthetic social environment

HOMEWORK

- Family Problems Inventory
- Child-proofing the home

REVIEW OF EVENTS SINCE THE EVALUATION

At the beginning of every session the parents are invited to describe any significant events that have transpired since the parents last met with the therapist. In the first session this will have been in most cases the time of the child's initial clinical evaluation. In some cases, the family will have been seeing the therapist regularly in ongoing treatment, the focus of which is now shifting to direct instruction in child management skills. Since each session begins with this review of prior events, it will receive no further discussion in the description of subsequent steps in the program.

OPEN DISCUSSION OF PARENTS' VIEWS OF THE CAUSES OF MISBEHAVIOR

Although it will be a major goal of this session to provide parents with a framework in which to understand child misbehavior and psychopathology, it is useful to assess the parents' perceptions of why children develop significant behavioral problems. Initially, you should invite parents to discuss openly what causes they believe lead to misbehavior in their children. These should be written down so that they can be placed within the model of causes of misbehavior to be presented later. In my experience, parents are quick to identify "getting attention" as a major reason children display disruptive behavior. While this is correct in some instances, you will later show how coercive interactions actually develop from escape/avoidance learning (negative reinforcement) in children rather than merely to get adult attention. Other parents will blame themselves, identifying "poor parenting" as a major cause of noncompliance. For now, simply note this comment, but be sure to respond to it later after explaining the model of misbehavior below. At that point, you will want to partially dispel this notion by showing how complex the causes of misbehavior can be. A few parents will correctly note that some children seem destined at birth to have behavioral difficulties; inviting parents to elaborate on this theme is a helpful transition into your presentation of the model below.

A MODEL FOR UNDERSTANDING CHILD MISBEHAVIOR

While research in child development and psychopathology has identified myriad causes of child misbehavior, they can be grouped into four major factors to ease teaching them to parents.

THE CHILD'S CHARACTERISTICS

Some children are born with a certain predilection toward deviant behavior and psychopathology. Such children may have *inherited predispositions* toward thought disorders, psychotic behavior, and intellectual delay, as well as attention deficits and impulsivity, to name but a few, given the evidence presently available on the familial nature of these disorders. Other children appear to manifest *difficult temperaments* that, very early in their development, bring them into conflict with their care-givers. Temperament here refers to the children's activity level, general attention span, emotionality, sociability, response to stimulation, and habit regularity. You should provide parents with the first handout for this step for them to follow in this discussion. Be sure to explain that these aspects of temperament appear to be inborn characteristics of the children to a great extent, are often easily identifiable within the first 6 months of life, and are stable over years of time.

Each characteristic should be briefly explained. After each, have parents indicate on the handout whether that characteristic is problematic for their child. *Activity level* here refers to the specific level of motor activity shown by the child. *Attention span* refers to the average duration of time a child usually spends watching, listening to, manipulating, or otherwise behaving toward stimuli in the environment. *Impulse control* refers to the child's ability to stop and think before he or she acts. Often children are trained to be more reflective, to consider the consequences of their actions before behaving. Some children, however, have great difficulty in inhibiting immediate responses, placing them at much greater risk for behavior management conflicts with their caregivers. *Emotionality* describes the child's general emotional reactions to events within the environment. Some children are generally irritable, cry often, are hard to console when upset, and emote very easily and often to excess. *Sociability* refers to the child's general level of interest in others as opposed to things. Eye contact with others, initiating interactions toward others, and generally viewing others as more important things to interact with in a situation than are objects are all aspects of sociability in children. *Response to stimulation* is used to capture the child's general reaction to tactile, auditory, or visual stimulation, noise, movement produced by others, and so forth. Some children withdraw when only slightly stimulated by their environment. Others may cry easily when stimulated. Others still may seek out stimulation, explore novel aspects of an environment vigorously, and in some cases enjoy mild stimulation from others. Finally, *habit regularity* refers to the consistency of the child's biological habits, such as eating, sleeping, and elimination patterns. Some children are fussy or picky eaters, develop colic easily, have shorter-than-normal sleep patterns, or have irregular habits of elimination. Obviously, these can add additional stress to care-givers in trying to establish an infant or young child's "routine."

Explain to parents that these are overlapping features of children and are simply lumped together into one general impression of a child's temperament. The greater a child deviates from normal on these dimensions of temperament and the more dimensions on which he or she is deviant, the greater is the likelihood of conflict developing with the parents. Such parent–child conflicts will often be greatest for the parent who must make the most daily demands on the child. Such demands are more likely to elicit the child's negative temperament, resulting in that parent having a far more negative view of the child's manageability than the parent having fewer daily management encounters with the child. It is not hard to see how this could lead to marital strife, with one parent carrying a greater brunt of the child's negative temperament than the other.

It is also not difficult to see how such child characteristics could lead to conflict with other adults and the community in which the child resides. In a society that values controlled, well-channeled activity levels, sustained attention, reasonably regulated emotional reactions, moderate degrees of sociability, curiosity evinced in healthy but channeled ways, and predictable regularity of habits that lend to easy caretaking, an infant or child who is seriously deviant or negative in these areas is destined to have great difficulties in social and familial adjustment.

Physical characteristics are another feature that may predispose children toward misbehavior. The child's physical appearance, motor coordination, strength, stamina, and general physical abilities are well-recognized factors in determining to some degree how others will react to them, at least initially. A child who is unattractive, incoordinated, weak, or generally different from others in physical abilities will have less positive initial interactions with others, may accidentally damage property, may be unable to participate gracefully in children's play or games, and may be at risk for failure in certain academic areas (e.g., handwriting). Such problems not only result in initial rejection, dislike, or outright hostility toward the child so afflicted but can render damage to the child's self-esteem and desire to be accepted by his or her family, peers, and society. The mere fact that a child may resemble someone else in the family who was disliked (a former husband, for instance) may subtly affect the types and manner of interactions with other family members (the mother in this case).

Finally, a child's *developmental abilities* may place the child at risk for behavioral problems. Like physical characteristics, developmental competencies also affect how others initially perceive children and subsequently interact with them. For instance, a mild delay in language development, impaired speech expression, less-than-average intellect, or poor visual–motor coordination may result in poor social acceptance, teasing, or other forms of social maltreatment. Such delays may also affect a child's social problem-solving abilities, ability to understand and comply with parental commands and requests, or ability to learn appropriate habits or emotional control. These may lead directly to conflict with care-givers and others with whom the child interacts. Parents should be invited to give examples in each of these areas as to specific characteristics they may have noted that affect children's social behavior and acceptance.

At this point, ask the parents to give a brief profile of their child in each of these areas in order to see what factors the child may already have that could predispose him or her toward misconduct. Use the child characteristics profile provided with the printed handouts that accompany this manual.

THE PARENTS' CHARACTERISTICS

You should now discuss with the parents the fact that their own characteristics play some role in the development or maintenance of behavior problems in their children. Following the same outline of characteristics used above in describing the behavior problem child, discuss how parents may have certain inherited predispositions to personal psychological disorders, temperamental characteristics, physical features or disabilities, or developmental disabilities that place them at risk for contributing to behavioral difficulties in their children. This seems to occur as a result of the effects of these characteristics on the parents' consistency and effectiveness in managing child misbehavior when it arises. Virtually the same difficulties that may plague the behavior problem child in these areas can also be seen in some parents. Parents are then encouraged to provide within these categories specific characteristics that they recognize may contribute to the problems parents have managing children, especially those with behavioral disorders. Then have the parents complete the parent characteristics profile that accompanies the handouts with this manual. The intent of the parent and child profiles is to make parents more cognizant of the fit between their own and their child's characteristics and to note where conflicts between them may arise. Also, parents may strive to modify their own characteristics where possible, or at least preclude them from exacerbating their management problems with the child by keeping them in mind as they raise this child.

SITUATIONAL CONSEQUENCES

Probably one of the most important factors contributing to child behavioral disorders are the consequences that occur in families because of inappropriate behavior by the child. In fact, it is through these consequences, particularly those provided by the parents, that several of the other factors described in this model operate. It appears that parent characteristics and family stress events operate directly on the ability of parents to provide consistent, appropriate, and effective consequences during the management of child behavior. Child characteristics certainly affect the manner in which the child reacts to these management efforts and hence indirectly affect the consequences the parents will subsequently employ to deal with the child's reactions.

Describe for the parents the notion that children do not behave without cause or reason; that is, child behavior is not random but occurs because of particular response predispositions of the child (the characteristics described above), his or her learning history within the family, and the consequences occurring in the immediate situation in which the problem behavior arises. The processes whereby these consequences operate can be subdivided into two fundamental concepts: positive reinforcement and escape/avoidance learning. These processes were discussed in chapter 1 and should be presented to the parents in language that is readily understandable to them.

Essentially, parents are taught that children may misbehave to gain positive consequences or rewards, or to escape from ongoing unpleasant, boring, or effortful activities. Parents are asked to describe the types of positive consequences that may accrue to childen for misbehavior. Most parents are quite capable of providing a rather accurate list of such consequences. They appear to have somewhat greater difficulty generating a list of consequences that children might wish to avoid, and so your assistance here may be necessary. Point out to parents that most of the activities we assign children to do, especially chores, are not especially pleasant, often require extended effort, and require the child to stop what he or she was doing (usually something enjoyable) to do this unpleasant activity. As a result, children may experiment with ways of escaping from or avoiding chores by developing oppositional behavior toward parent commands. You may find it helpful to show the schematic diagram of a noncompliant interaction from Figure 1.1 and describe it in some detail so parents can appreciate how consequences they are providing for oppositional behavior are serving to create and sustain it.

Explain that a child need not be successful all the time in gaining positive consequences or avoiding unpleasant activities in order to show disruptive, noncompliant, or oppositional behavior to most commands. This is the principle of intermittent reinforcement, and as most therapists know, such partial schedules of consequences can strengthen and sustain noncompliance in children even though the child succeeds with such behavior only a minority of the time. Sometimes using the example of adult gambling and how it is maintained by small intermittent payoffs helps to convey this notion to parents. Again, teaching the jargon is not so important as conveying the principle or concept to the parents.

FAMILY STRESS

Now you should review with the parents a variety of potential stress events that families may experience. These can be subdivided into stressors related to personal problems, the marital relationship, health problems, financial problems, stress related to one or both spouses' occupations, problems with relatives and friends, and problems created by siblings.

Parents should be taught that these stress events can act in several ways to increase the likelihood of noncompliant or inappropriate behavior in children. First, because they directly affect the parents' own emotional well-being, they will certainly affect how effectively and consistently parents will deal with unacceptable behavior when it occurs. Parents may fluctuate in their management tactics much more when under stress. On one hand, they may increase their commands, supervision, and punishment of a child because of their own irritable mood. On the other hand, they may withdraw from managing the child's behavior because of preoccupation with the stress events and the anxiety and depression that may accompany them. Either way, parental management of children becomes far more variable and inconsistent, leading to greater success of child oppositional behavior in escaping or avoiding unpleasant or effortful tasks.

A second way in which family stress affects child misbehavior is by altering parental perceptions of the child. Depressed, anxious, or distressed parents tend to exaggerate their reports of child behavior problems. Should parents act on these perceptions, which they typically do, then they will behave as if the child's behavior were deviant or unacceptable when in fact it is not. In so doing, parents may inadvertently punish normal or acceptable child behavior, increase their commands, directiveness, and general negativism toward children, and begin using negative words to describe a child's character or personality, which can affect not only child behavior but self-esteem. This may lead to deviant behavior by the child where none previously existed, confirming the parents' initial perception that the child was deviant.

A third way in which family stress increases misbehavior in children is by its direct effects on children and their emotional well-being. Like the parents, children can become preoccupied with family stress events, and these create anxiety, depression, or distress. These reactions may then heighten the likelihood of the child's displaying negative, oppositional, or noncompliant behavior.

You must help parents appreciate the role of family stress in creating or exacerbating child misbehavior. Marital discord, family financial troubles, tense relations with relatives, and so forth, can all create an emotional climate in the home in which child oppositional behavior may flourish. Certainly, the parents cannot be expected to solve all of the potential stress events immediately, but they should be encouraged to begin making plans for how they intend to reduce the stress created by a particular stressor in the family. Many times parents have simply chosen to accept their fate and live with whatever stressors may be occurring even though efforts can be made to try to resolve them. At the very least, parents need to become aware that such stressors are affecting their management of the child and take steps to see that such an influence on their management is reduced. To help initiate this process, one of the homework assignments for the parents will be to complete the Family Problems Inventory so you can take stock of potential stressors and start proposing solutions to them where feasible.

THE RECIPROCAL INTERACTION AMONG THESE FACTORS

You should now briefly explain to the parents that while each of the above factors contributes directly to creating or sustaining noncompliant behavior in children, it can also influence each of the other factors, resulting in even further difficulties in the family. For instance, medical problems of either a parent or child can influence the family financial situation, which itself may then affect the parents' marital relationship. This feeds back to exacerbate child misbehavior. This can create a veritable cauldron of risk events within families that may, over time, foment even greater behavioral problems with the child.

THE GOAL OF THERAPY: ENGINEERING A "BEST FIT"

At this point, it is helpful to summarize the foregoing presentation by saying that many times the characteristics of the parent and child are such that each will naturally prove irritating to the other. Similarly, certain parent or child characteristics may not react well to certain family stress events, which further bring out the deviant parent or child characteristic and increase deviant behavior in both parties. One goal of therapy is to try to change these poorly fitting situational, parental, and child characteristics where possible, so as to lessen the behavioral problems of the child. This can be achieved through showing parents how to

1. Recognize their own "risk" factors and change them where possible, or at least try to prevent them from interfering with their effective management of their child.
2. Recognize certain "risk" factors in the child, attempt to change them where feasible, and at least learn to accept those that cannot be changed and strive to cope with them as best as possible.
3. Change the situational consequences they are providing that may be serving to create, maintain, or exacerbate child noncompliance.

THE NEED FOR A PROSTHETIC
SOCIAL ENVIRONMENT

For parents of children having mild behavior problems or oppositional behavior, it is very possible that this program will bring their child's behavior back within the normally accepted range of social conduct. In other words, the problems for which the family sought help can be "cured." However, with more serious behavioral problems, such as those experienced by hyperactive or attention deficit disorder children and children with pervasive developmental disorders or psychosis, this parent training program will not "cure" the disorders. Instead, it will greatly reduce the distress the parents and child experience over the child's disruptive, noncompliant, and generally unacceptable behavior. In such cases, parent training can create a long-term, ongoing, prosthetic social environment for the child that maximizes his or her ability to behave appropriately. Even at their best, such children will certainly have more difficulties with familial and social conduct than normal children; however, they need not experience the level of deviant behavior often seen at the time of referral. A corollary of this is that such children *need* these methods if they are to do what normal children appear to be able to accomplish without help. Like a mechanical prosthetic limb, these behavior management techniques will serve to permit the behaviorally handicapped child to become more normal. Remove the prosthetic techniques, and the child may well revert to previous deviant behavior. It may eventually be possible, however, to gradually reduce the frequency, intensity, and systematic usage of these behavioral methods over long intervals as the child matures and gains greater self-control so that the gains of therapy are maintained.

Explain the above issues that apply to the particular child and circumstances. Here also a strong case should be made for the role of parental motivation in the treatment program. No matter how effective for others, these techniques must be applied by the parents or will be no help. Stress that you cannot do it for the parents; they must practice and implement the procedures themselves if any real hope of changing the child is to be realized.

HOMEWORK

There are two homework assignments for this session. First, the parents are to complete the Family Problems Inventory over the next week. Encourage each parent to complete one separately. They need not share their answers with their spouse if they choose not to, but where this occurs it is obvious evidence of marital disharmony. The parents are to list briefly the stress events occurring under each category and then propose what, if anything, they intend to do about it. They do not have to solve their problems this week, but they should at least formulate plans to reduce those stressors noted. I am often surprised to find that material is divulged on the inventory that was not revealed in the initial evaluation of the family, now that the parents can appreciate the role of such stressors in child misbehavior. For families receiving training in a group, you should state that the contents of their inventory will not be shared with the rest of the parent group when it is turned in at the next class. Instead, you will review it privately and speak with the parents about any significant stressors that may deserve more immediate attention. Occasionally, an issue is revealed that results in training being temporarily postponed while that issue is addressed. For families receiving individual training, review the inventory with the parents at the beginning of the next session.

The second assignment is to have the parents child-proof their home if they have not already done so. Research indicates that behavior problem children are more accident prone, more likely to damage property and valuables, and more likely to create accidents for others than are normal children. Parents should be encouraged to review each room in their home for potentially harmful agents or machines, for valuable property that could inadvertently be damaged by the young child, or for items that the parents wish to preserve or protect that are now within easy reach of the impulsive child.

Pay Attention!

1. To educate parents in how the style of their interactions with their children greatly affects their children's motivation to work for them.
2. To train parents in methods of attending to positive child behavior while differentially ignoring negative behavior.
3. To require parents to practice these differential attending skills at home over the next week.
4. To begin establishing a more positive interaction pattern between parent and child.

MATERIALS REQUIRED

- Home Situations Questionnaire
- Parent handouts
    Paying Attention to Your Child's Good Play Behavior
    Suggestions for Giving Positive Feedback and Approval to Your Child

STEP OUTLINE

- Review of homework
- Parents complete the Home Situations Questionnaire
- Rationale for developing attending skills
    Importance of quality of attention to people
    Parents discuss "good" versus "bad" supervisor
    Discussion of how parents attend to problem child
- Goals of this session

- Distribute and review parent handout on attending skills
    Important features of the skills in handout
    Parental reactions to the technique
- Model the technique for parents
- Parents practice methods in session
- Determine when special time will be done at home

HOMEWORK
- Daily special time practice periods
- Record special time practice

This session begins with a review of the previous session's homework assignments and of any problems encountered in completing the Family Problems Inventory. You may wish to review the contents of the Family Problems Inventory should the program be provided on an individual basis to a family. If it is a parent group, these questionnaires are set aside for later review by you outside of the parent group. You should then give the parents the Home Situations Questionnaire to complete again to permit the periodic assessment of progress in treating the child's behavior. Little, if any, improvement in these ratings is expected, compared to those of the initial assessment. For now, set these ratings aside in the child's chart for comparison with later ratings on this scale. The scale will be completed again at the beginning of Step 4.

INTRODUCING THE RATIONALE FOR DEVELOPING ATTENDING SKILLS

DO NOT provide the parents with the handout for this session until discussion has occurred on the quality of attention and how it affects people's behavior. Parents should initially be questioned as to whether they believe receiving attention from others is valuable to them. This should then lead to a discussion of how the quality of the attention we receive from a person affects our subsequent desire to work with that person.

In these discussions, I have found the following technique particularly useful. I ask parents to put aside for the moment any thoughts about their children and concentrate on individuals with whom the parents have worked. Specifically, parents are asked to think about the worst person with whom they have ever worked, usually a past supervisor, and to try to describe what were the characteristics of that person that led to those feelings. Have the parents divide a sheet of paper in half with a line running vertically down the page. In the right-hand column, they are to write at least five characteristics that made this the worst person with whom they have worked. If this is a parent group, use a blackboard and record the answers given by the parents on the board. Parents usually have little difficulty thinking of these characteristics, but if they should, assistance can be provided. Take time to get the parents to specify the feelings they had toward this person because of the undesirable ways in which they were treated.

After these characteristics are discussed, the parents are instructed to imagine the best person with whom they have worked. They are to record at least five characteristics that made this person good to work with. These responses are recorded in the left-hand column of the paper. Again, answers from parents in a parent training group can be recorded on a blackboard. At this point, the parents are asked which person they are most like in their interactions with the behavior problem child. Most parents honestly report that they are more often like the worst supervisor than the best supervisor in this exercise. Time should be taken to discuss how their child might come to feel as they did about working for such a person. It is possible that the child may have, in a behavioral sense, gone "on strike" or created a "work slowdown" because of the poor management and work conditions in the home.

OBJECTIVES OF THE SESSION

Having introduced the notion that the quality of our work for others and the way we feel toward them is greatly determined by the way in which they interact or "attend" to us, you should now review the objectives of this session with the parents. Primary among these is the need, demonstrated in the exercise above, to improve the quality of parental attention given to the behavior disordered child. Granted, improving that attention is unlikely to be sufficient to completely ameliorate the problems with this child, but it is a necessary first step in that process. In addition, as noted in an earlier chapter, the reward value to children of parental attention in families with behavior problem children is generally lower than that in normal families.

Hence, if parental attention is to be used to improve child compliance, it must first be enhanced in value. The methods to be introduced here will contribute to that goal.

A second purpose of this session is to improve the general relations between parent and child through the use of the nondirective play practice periods to be done for homework. This leads the child to feel that the parents are interested in him or her, even if the child has behaved badly during the day. This is done in order to reverse the progressive trend, often seen in such families, of the parents spending less time in leisure activities with the problem child. In other words, the play procedures in this session are designed to get parents and children interacting more positively toward each other more often than was previously the case. Many parents report a renewed sense of pleasure in playing with the child following these guidelines, and we believe the children come to feel the same, given their frequent requests for additional such play periods once they are begun. While such a goal may seem overly ambitious to parents at this stage of training, it is often noted at the end of even one week of conducting these special playtimes that the parents find the children more desirable persons with whom to interact, and vice versa.

A third objective of this step is to get parents to begin differentially attending to positive child behaviors while ignoring negative ones. This is often contrary to the parents' current practice of ignoring positive child behaviors and attending or responding only to the disruptive or negative ones. Each of these objectives should be described to the parents to insure that they fully understand the rationale for the play technique discussed in the parent handout.

REVIEWING THE PARENT HANDOUT

The handout for Step 2 should now be distributed for the parents to read. Afterwards, review the important points of the handout in some detail. As the handout indicates, this session is designed to train parents in using new methods of paying attention to child behaviors during play. The handout instructs parents to select a time when their children are playing in an activity that the children normally enjoy and that is appropriate. Parents are then to approach the children and begin a period of 15 to 20 minutes of playing with the children in the manner discussed in the handout. Parents are encouraged to make this "special time" an even more formal activity by telling the child that the parent will henceforth be taking time each day to play with the child. The child is then asked what activity he or she would like to do around the home that day for the special time. The children are permitted to choose the activity, within reason. It is essential that children select the activity so that they come to believe that their parents are interested in what the children want to do and not in simply taking charge of the play and redirecting it to something that the parents desire to do.

As suggested in the handout, it is critical that the parents learn to relax during this time and that they have absolutely nothing else on their minds other than learning to attend to what the children are doing. For this reason, parents should not attempt to play with the children immediately before going out on an errand or shopping trip, as it is likely that the quality of the attention provided by the parent would be quite superficial. It is the sole purpose of this playtime to practice attending positively to ongoing child behaviors.

During the playtime, the parents should watch, mentally note, and follow the children's various activities for a few moments before beginning to narrate what the children are doing. This narrative description should occur occasionally throughout the playtime. The children will begin to develop the idea that the parents are quite interested in what they do, regardless of how trivial or simple it may seem. In addition, narration of the children's activities necessarily precludes the parents from asking intrusive questions or giving commands in such a way that they come to take charge of the play activities. As noted in the handout, parents are, if possible, to avoid giving any commands or questions during this time.

One method for teaching parents to adopt this style of narration is to have them imagine that they are a sportscaster describing the action of a sporting event for a radio broadcast. The description should be interesting, detailed, and generally a running, uncritical commentary on the events taking place. Depending upon the way in which the parents choose to narrate and the degree to which this narration is embellished with cues of interest and excitement, this style of paying attention to child behavior can be highly effective at reinforcing the children for appropriate play activities. I have found that younger children appreciate this narrative more than older children, who come to find it disruptive of their play activities and somewhat condescending. Parents should therefore exercise their judgment as to how much narration to employ with a child. The important point here, regardless of the children's age, is to have the parents spend time with the children without criticizing, directing, or controlling the children's behavior but watching and appreciating what the children do.

As noted above, it is essential that the parents limit their questioning and eliminate any commands that may be given during this time. Commands are obviously designed to take control over an activity, and such control is to be inhibited during the children's playtime. Parents should be told that there is virtually nothing that they need to teach during this playtime that could not be deferred for teaching during some other time. Even if the children's play is not up to the standards expected by the parents, the parents should avoid taking charge of the play and trying to teach the children different ways of playing. Questions, like commands, are also intrusive upon children's play; they necessitate that the children redirect their activities in order to respond to the parents. Again, this is to be avoided during the special playtime as much as possible. Older children may require somewhat more questioning during these play activities and may not find it as intrusive as younger children. Furthermore, the kinds of questions asked of younger children are often superfluous since the parent often knows the answer already but is using the question to quiz the child as to how much they have learned in their development so far.

Throughout the playtime, the parents should intersperse various comments of positive, genuine feedback. As noted in the handout, this feedback is not necessarily glowing praise for what the children are doing. Instead, it is simply a statement that reflects the parents' interest in what the children are doing and perhaps the parents' enjoyment of being with the children. A list of positive phrases that parents may use during play is the second handout to be given as part of this session. We provide this handout to parents so that they do not come to use only one or two well-worn phrases of appreciation during this special time. Parents are taught that positive feedback can be given not only verbally, but through physical gestures communicating liking and appreciation. Praise, when given, should be quite specific and can emphasize not only what the children are doing that is acceptable but what they are not doing that is unacceptable. Parents should be quite specific as to the behavior they are appreciating, rather than utilizing vague references, such as "good boy" or "nice girl." It is believed that such specificity increases the effectiveness of praise as a reinforcer for a given child behavior.

Many parents ask at this point how they should behave during the special playtime if their children begin to become seriously disruptive. It is my belief that the parents' best reaction is to simply turn away momentarily from the child in an effort to ignore it. Often, this readily reduces misbehavior. Should the unacceptable behavior escalate, however, the parents should merely tell the child that the special time has ended and that it can resume again later once the child is behaving appropriately. On rare occasions, the level of misbehavior will be such that it is deserving of punishment. As this point, the parents are instructed to handle the disciplining in a manner similar to the way in which they have been handling it previously. No effort should be made here to introduce the concept of time out from reinforcement. Parents should be told that misbehavior during special time is quite rare in our experience. This probably has to do with the fact that the child is being given no commands, which often serve as prompts to the child to misbehave or act in an oppositional manner.

You should note that the special playtime is to be conducted alone with the behavior disordered child and without siblings or the spouse interfering. If necessary, such special time can be given to the other children in the family at another time of day, but the time with the problem child is always to be on a one-to-one basis. This certainly precludes the problem child from sharing special playtime with siblings whose behaviors and characteristics may be more desirable than his or her own and hence more likely to attract parental praise and attention away from the problem child. Where two parents are present, one can take the siblings away to another room for activities while the second practices the special attending methods during play with the problem child. After 15 to 20 minutes, the parents can change their respective roles, giving both a chance to practice these attending skills.

COMMON PARENTAL REACTIONS TO THESE METHODS

Parents should be provided ample time to discuss any concerns or reactions they have to this method. Often, parents note that they have not had time to do such playing with the child since the birth of younger siblings into the family. One particular reaction common at this point is the remark that the play techniques seem especially simple and will be quite easy to implement. Such is not the case, as noted at the bottom of the handout. Inhibiting commands and questions, concentrating on positive narration, and providing occasional feedback take considerable practice to do well. The elimination of commands and questions is quite difficult for many parents, as they are accustomed to controlling their children's behavior much of the day via these mechanisms. Parents often find themselves at a loss for what to say during playtime once these social devices have been forbidden by the therapist. Instruction can provide ways to translate questions into comments or reflective remarks by parents.

Another reaction often heard from parents is that the special time does not seem directed at the problems for which they sought treatment. It is hoped that this issue will have been handled by the exercise at the beginning of the session comparing qualities of good versus bad supervisors. If not, then you can reiterate here the need for parents to improve the quality and value of their attending skills with children before such attention can be used to increase child compliance to commands. The need to rebuild the parent–child relationship should be made obvious. The fact that this method can contribute to that process is often supported by the observation that most children so treated have requested that the playtime continue beyond its usual stopping point—clearly a sign that the child finds the parents' newly developing attending skills to be quite reinforcing.

Some parents comment that if they spend special time with the children that is filled with praise and appreciation, the children will come to expect such treatment for everything they do. There are several ways to handle such remarks. First, it can be pointed out that this has not happened with the thousands of families treated under this program to date. Second, it is helpful to explore with the parents the basis for this attitude toward child behaviors. Obviously, the parents are being paid by an employer for their own work, which is in a sense a similar way of reinforcing them for their performance on the job. Without such payment, few parents would return to work. Furthermore, most parents expect a certain amount of gratitude from their spouse, as well as older children, for the everyday responsibilities they handle for the family. Like the child, they too desire the appreciation and recognition of others for what they do within the family. In short, the child desires attention the same way parents do.

Many marriages have floundered because the spouse felt "taken for granted," which is merely another way of saying that contributions to the marriage were unappreciated.

Some parents may note that they are too busy for this sort of activity. The remark conveys the essence of an important problem in such families, that there is little time or importance assigned to child rearing. Is it any wonder behavior problems in the children have emerged from such a family interaction pattern? I have sometimes responded to such remarks, half humorously, by suggesting that the parents consider putting the children up for adoption if they are unable to find even 15 minutes in their day for a child.

MODELING AND PRACTICING THE METHODS

If the child is available in the session, you can take the child to a corner of the room and begin playing with the child, with the parents observing the activities. The therapist models the appropriate methods, taking care to make an occasional mistake that can then be discussed with the parents later in the session. Resources permitting, a therapist may wish to videotape such a play session with a child to show to other parents undergoing training in this session. Thereafter, the parents should practice the attending skills in front of the therapist, with appropriate feedback being provided by the therapist. Where the child is unavailable, parents can role-play the play situation with your assistance.

Afterwards, the parents should review with you the feelings they have about these methods. Many parents respond that they did not believe the method was as difficult as it proved to be in reality. Parents should then discuss how they intend to implement the daily special times at home during the coming week(s). They should be encouraged to choose a particular time of day that is best for both parent and child, perhaps when other siblings are occupied with their own activities. Where possible, each parent is to practice the attending skills daily with the child. For older children, it may not be as helpful to have a formal time set aside each day, since such children may often be involved with various out-of-home activities or school homework. In such cases, parents should watch throughout the day for times that seem opportune to approach and interact with the child over some play activity in which he or she is currently engaged. Watching television together is discouraged since verbal narration or discussion during that activity is often annoying or intrusive.

If the child chooses a competitive game, parents should allow the child to invent new rules or even cheat in the game without recrimination during this playtime. Parents should remember that the purpose of the time is not to learn how to properly play a game, but to practice their skills in attending to the child. Nonetheless, cooperative games and activities lend themselves better to this special time than do competitive ones.

Care should be taken to explain to the parents that this special playtime is not going to miraculously cure all of the child's behavioral problems. In fact, noncompliance by the child during the subsequent week is often unabated since it is mostly in reaction to parental commands rather than such special play periods. What the parents can expect, however, is that the child may come to view the parents as more desirable people with whom to interact and work. This may not occur for some families, but most report a slight improvement in their relationship with the child after only one week. Parents should also be told that this special playtime is to become a part of the household routine for an indefinite period of time. After the first week of practice, the parents can reduce the frequency of special time with the child to three or four times per week but should strive to maintain this frequency indefinitely.

HOMEWORK

Parents are instructed in the homework for the coming week. They are to practice the attending skills during special time on a daily basis, where possible. They should record a few sentences in a diary as to what they did during each day's special time and how the child reacted. Parents may wish to note special problems they encountered with the methods, to discuss during the next training session. By assigning this as homework, parents are more likely to practice the procedures, since they are more accountable for their week's activities with the child.

STEP THREE

Increasing Compliance
to Commands and Requests

GOALS

1. To train parents to use effective attending skills to increase immediate child compliance to parental commands.
2. To increase the effectiveness of parental commands at eliciting child compliance.

MATERIALS REQUIRED

- Parent handouts
    Paying Attention to Your Child's Compliance
    How to Give Effective Commands

STEP OUTLINE

- Review of homework
    Parents' use of special attending skills
    Reminder to continue special time periods with child
- Extension of attending skills from play to compliance
- Ways of increasing effectiveness of commands
- Use of compliance training periods
- Parental reactions to methods
- Model methods for parents
- Parents practice attending to compliance
- Critique parental practice

HOMEWORK
- Continue special time periods with child
- Praising and attending to compliance
- Daily compliance training periods

The parents' records of their special playtime activities should be reviewed. If parents failed to do the assignment, no new material is presented. Instead, the reason for this failure is addressed, and the parents are requested to try it again during the coming week. Otherwise, you should instruct the parents that they are to continue the special playtimes with the child indefinitely on a frequency of three to four times per week. This will (1) produce further improvements in the parent–child relationship, (2) allow the child to continue to receive moments of positive attention from parents despite what may be a day filled with difficult child behavior, and (3) build child self-esteem.

Some parents comment that their children appeared to be both pleasantly surprised and dismayed at the new attention they were receiving from their parents. A few children may have even questioned the parents as to a hidden motive for this unexpected positive attention. After the initial surprise has passed, many children settle easily into the routine of the daily special playtimes, often reminding their parents of the commitment the parents made to them about taking such time, should the parents forget. Many of the children request that the playtime continue beyond its normal 15- to 20-minute limit. A few parents seem pleasantly surprised that their children find them to be so desirable after years of oppositional behavior and arguments from the children. Some parents will have found no change in their children's behavior. They should be told not to be discouraged as the method may take longer to yield benefits for some children, especially if the history of negative parent–child relations has been a long and difficult one for both parties. A few parents complain that while the children appeared to enjoy the play periods, they did not expressly thank the parents for having taken the time to be with them. These parents should be instructed that the important thing is that the children received the attention, not that they expressly acknowledge it. The true impact of the play period will be judged in the weeks to come as a result of its effects on the parents' own attending skills and on the parent–child relationship.

EXTENSION OF ATTENDING SKILLS FROM PLAY TO COMPLIANCE

Provide the parents with the first handout for this session. The handout is brief and should be easily understood by most parents. Essentially, parents are to "catch their children being good" and to respond to compliance with attention, appreciation, and praise. The purpose of the session is to teach parents to increase compliance to commands by providing positive consequences, in this case parental attention, contingent upon child compliance with commands. Parents are instructed to pay particular attention this week when they issue commands to their children. At these times, they are to remain in the area where compliance is to be carried out, watch, narrate, and appreciate the compliant activities of the child. In many cases, parents issue commands and then depart the area to attend to other matters, returning periodically to see if the task has been done. This session instructs parents to remain near the child during compliance so as to provide ongoing positive attention and comments about the child's compliance. Statements of praise and appreciation should be quite specific as to what the parents find positive in the child's behavior, such as "I like it when you do as I say," or "Mom really likes it when you pick up your toys." Parents often find little difficulty with understanding this concept. Actually increasing their praise of child compliance is another matter and will take practice.

Parents should be instructed to provide particularly salient positive attention and rewards to a child who has complied with a household rule or routine chore without having been instructed to do so, particularly when the child previously was noncompliant with that rule or chore. It is believed that this increases the likelihood of the child internalizing such rules and routines and complying with them in future situations.

GIVING EFFECTIVE COMMANDS

You can now provide the second handout for this session, dealing with methods for improving the effectiveness of parental commands. These are straightforward recommendations that can be briefly commented upon by the therapist. First, the parents should be sure that they mean the command they are about to give and are willing to see the task to its completion. Second, the command should be presented as a direct statement, not a favor or a question. It need not be presented in a negative tone of voice, but it should be clear to the child that the parent is serious about the task. Third, parents should give simple commands rather than multiple ones when dealing with the behavior disordered child. Adequate time should be allotted to see that the first request has been obeyed before issuing a subsequent command. Fourth, parents should make eye contact with the child. Yelling out commands to a child from an adjoining room is not helpful. Parents should look directly at the child to insure his or her undivided attention. Fifth, parents should reduce significant distractions in the area before initiating a command. For instance, if the child is watching television, playing a video game, or listening to a stereo system, the parent should turn the apparatus off or direct the child to do so before assigning the task to be done. Parents are unlikely to have much success competing with these highly stimulating and engaging devices. Sixth, where necessary, have the child repeat the command back to the parent to insure the child has understood the request and to reinforce the memory of the command. Finally, parents may wish to assign time limits to extended tasks, such as cleaning a bedroom or doing homework. In this case, the parents should set a specified time on a kitchen timer and let the child know the time limits and consequences. For a protracted task, it may also prove helpful to write a list of task steps for the child to carry during the performance of the job. This insures that there can be no debate over what the components were in the task.

ESTABLISHING COMPLIANCE TRAINING PERIODS

In teaching any new behavior or increasing the occurrence of one already present in a child's repertoire, the rate of acquisition or the increase in the desired behavior is related to the number of training opportunities available for reinforcing that behavior. In view of this principle, we have found it useful to have parents actually increase their rate of commands to a child during a brief training period so as to permit more opportunities for reinforcing compliance to requests. These compliance training periods should last about 3 to 5 minutes, and parents should have at least two or three each day. During these periods, parents should ask the child to perform a series of simple requests, each of which requires minimal effort by the child, such as "Hand me that magazine," "Come here and let me tuck in your shirt/ blouse," or "Please get me the salt shaker." Such commands are less likely to meet with oppositional behavior because they involve minimal work by the children. Parents are to use this time to expressly attend to, praise, and otherwise reward the child for compliance. For very young children, a small taste of a favorite snack food or drink can be given during this time for compliance to some of the commands. For older children, appreciation will be sufficient for now. Parents should implement these training periods at times of the day when the child is not engaged in some special or desirable activity but appears to be between play activities, as this is likely to increase the probability of compliance.

You should review the parents' reactions to these methods, model the methods, and have the parents practice them in your presence.

COMMON PARENTAL REACTIONS

"What if the child fails to comply with my commands during this week?" Tell parents to handle the child's noncompliance as they typically have done. You are not yet ready to teach parents the disciplining procedures of this program, so do not get lulled into training discipline methods before the other steps have been mastered by the parents.

"What if the child does not comply with the commands I give during the special compliance training periods?" Tell parents to simply ignore the noncompliance for the moment and issue another brief command for the child to do something else for the parent.

"Praise has never motivated my child. Why should I expect it to work this week?" Although not as common as the other parental reactions noted here, this reaction sometimes occurs and often shows that the parent has not fully appreciated the lesson from Step 2— that some types of praise and attention are more valuable to children than others. It is likely that the parents have previously employed ineffective attending and praising skills; certainly they are unlikely to use them in the style being taught in this program. You can respond to these parents by indicating that the praise and attention you are asking them to try is likely to be different from what they have used previously and therefore may result in motivating their child. Even then, changing a child's behavior may take more than just 1 week of parental praising of the child, and so patience is required. Finally, such praise and attention will slowly begin to improve child self-esteem even though the changes in compliance are not dramatic or immediate. Such change in child self-esteem is a laudable goal in itself.

"Isn't giving commands in this way too harsh?" Some parents believe that giving commands as imperatives violates etiquette in that it lacks the courtesy of favors, requests, and other social kindnesses that should be used when asking others to do things for us. While such etiquette may be used with normally well-behaved children, it is highly unlikely to elicit compliance from clinic-referred noncompliant children. You should inform parents of this, saying that when the children become compliant, parents can return to using such social graces for the purpose of teaching proper etiquette. For now, it is essential that children first learn to comply with parental authority.

HOMEWORK

This week parents should try praising and appreciating the child when he or she complies with commands. They should further practice the methods for increasing the effectiveness of their commands and should implement two to three compliance training periods per day. The special time activities are to continue but need not be recorded by the parents.

Parents should be forewarned that simply increasing attention to compliance does not automatically increase compliant behavior in all children. For some children, the use of praise may have to be continued over long time periods before it is successful at improving compliance. For others, especially more deviant children, praise may not be sufficient as a reinforcer. Reassure parents that another, more potent reinforcement method will be taught in a later session. For now, they should try to use their praise and attention to encourage compliant behavior and improve child self-esteem.

Decreasing Disruptiveness— Increasing Independent Play

GOALS

1. To increase the use by parents of effective attending skills for independent, nondisruptive compliance by children.
2. To increase parental monitoring of child behavior in the home and neighborhood.

MATERIALS REQUIRED

- Home Situations Questionnaire
- Parent handout
   Paying Attention When Your Child Is Not Bothering You

STEP OUTLINE

- Review of homework
- Readminister the Home Situations Questionnaire
- Discuss how children disrupt their parents' activities
- Distribute parent handout on decreasing disruption and increasing independent play
- Model methods for parents
- Parents practice attending to independent play
- Parental reactions to methods
- Instruct parents to increase monitoring of child behavior

HOMEWORK

- Practicing attending to independent play
- Recording the practice sessions
- Increase monitoring of children's independent activities

As is customary, homework is reviewed for problems parents may be encountering in implementing previous methods. Many parents will report only slight increases in compliance with requests since the prior session. They should be told to continue attending to and praising compliant behavior, as it may take several weeks before such engrained behaviors as opposition or noncompliance, which have been successful for years for the child, will change. Other parents will note some improvement in their child, suggesting that such children are more sensitive to reinforcement by attention than the parents may have originally believed.

To assess again the child's response to treatment so far, have parents complete the Home Situations Questionnaire. Do not be surprised if there has been little change since the rating scale was given during the initial evaluation of the child.

DISCUSSION OF DISRUPTIVE BEHAVIOR BY CHILDREN

Before distributing the handout for this session, the therapist should engage the parents in a discussion of the specific kinds of disruptive behavior often seen in their child and why the parents believe this behavior persists. Parents often report that they are unable to talk on the telephone, speak with visitors in the home or with their spouse in the evening, read newspapers or magazines, or otherwise engage in a task without the behavior problem child disrupting them. Many parents will note that children do so in an effort to gain attention from parents, and this is certainly the case. But if parental attention is such a motivator of children's disruptive behavior then why don't children resist bothering their parents in order to get attention? The question should be posed to parents, for its answer is obvious—there is minimal attention paid in these families to children when they are playing or complying independently and not disrupting parental activities.

This situation is easily illustrated by using the example of talking on the telephone. Most parents of behavior problem children describe this situation as highly problematic for them because of child disruptiveness. The parents should be asked if they have ever temporarily interrupted their telephone conversation to yell at, reprimand, or discipline a child for disruption. Most, if not all, will answer in the affirmative. Then parents should be asked whether they have ever interrupted their conversation to praise or attend to a child for *not* disrupting the call but instead playing quietly nearby. Few, if any, parents will answer yes to such a question. The implication of this situation is that if children wish to receive parental attention, they are most successful at doing so through disruption of parental activity, particularly if that activity involves attention being paid to someone other than the child. Clearly, if the situation were reversed and parental attention were given for nondisruptive behavior, then children should decrease their disruptiveness and increase their playing independently of their parents.

DISTRIBUTE AND EXPLAIN THE PARENT HANDOUT

At this point, the parents should be provided with the handout for this session. Explain the method described in the handout, which is essentially a shaping procedure. The method involves having the parent initially attend to a child's nondisruptive behavior on a very frequent basis. Then the frequency of attention is gradually reduced as the child begins engaging in longer periods of not disrupting the parent while the parent is busy. When disruptions do occur by the child, they are to be ignored by the parent as much as possible.

You can illustrate the method by an example of a parent trying to read a magazine or cook a meal. In either case, the parent should always begin by assigning the child some activity to perform while the parent is busy or at least to stipulate that the child is not to bother the parent. For instance, the parent might say, "I want you to sit here and color in your book while I read this magazine. Do not interrupt me." The parent then begins reading the magazine but stops within a minute or so to praise the child for complying and not bothering the parent. The command is then reissued to the child, and the parent resumes reading. He or she then reads for a slightly longer interval, stopping again to praise the child for compliance. The parent returns to reading, this time for an even longer interval, after which the child is praised. Gradually, the intervals of reading are progressively lengthened before the parent provides further praise and attention to the child. For very young children, small tastes of a favorite snack food can be used periodically to reinforce this independent play.

A similar progression might be seen if the parent were attempting to prepare a meal. Once again, the child is directed to play away from the parent and assigned a particular play activity (e.g., watch television, color, or play with blocks). The parent then initiates the meal preparation but stops work frequently to praise the child. The intervals between reinforcements of the child are gradually lengthened until the child is able to play for 5 to 10 minutes (depending on developmental abilities) of sustained, nondisruptive activity, with parental attention given only at the end of the interval.

This takes some patience and organizational talent by the parents, but most can acquire this simple shaping procedure quite easily. Parents should remember that the initial purpose of the activity is not for them to read or cook but to watch and reinforce their child for not bothering them. As they gradually shape up the interval of time the child can play away from them, they will be able to read or perform some other activity uninterrupted.

MODELING AND PRACTICE OF METHODS

You can now model the method by taking the child to a playroom where the parent can observe you, as in prior sessions, and instruct the child to play with a toy while you read nearby. The child is told not to interrupt. Because children are more likely to obey you than their parents in such encounters, you should have little difficulty reinforcing compliance with such a request. You should sit nearby and read a few lines of a magazine before putting it down, approaching the child, and praising him or her for not interrupting the reading. Then return to reading for a slightly longer time interval, stop again and praise the child for playing alone, and continue reading. As above, the intervals of reading are gradually lengthened, with occasional reinforcement of the child. Parents are then to practice the procedure with your supervision.

COMMON PARENTAL REACTIONS

Parents often have several reactions to this method. First, many parents operate under the philosophy of "let sleeping dogs lie." This translates simply to not paying attention to their children when they are behaving quietly and appropriately, for fear that the parent attention will only spark new occurrences of undesirable behavior. In fact, such parents will often say that they have tried to reward their children previously for appropriate independent play, only to find that their rewards triggered new episodes of aversive or noncompliant behavior. Explain to these parents that when the independent play of their children is not rewarded, there is no reason to expect that it will recur with any greater frequency. In fact, it is likely to diminish over time because of the lack of reinforcement for its occurrence. Furthermore, tell these parents that the children are probably misbehaving when the parents attend to them because the children have learned that this is one method of keeping the parents in the room for greater lengths of time. If the children were to continue to play appropriately, the parents would likely leave the room again. Thus, these children have learned that when the parents come to praise them, the best way to sustain that parental attention is to begin to behave inappropriately. The technique taught in this session, by contrast, is to reward the children for independent play and to ignore them or leave the room when misbehavior occurs.

A second reaction of parents is to complain of not being able to finish their own activities if they must interrupt them frequently to attend to the child's independent play. While this may be true initially, after several days it is quite possible to teach a child to play independently for increasingly longer periods of time without disturbing the parent. The eventual result is that the child can play alone for the entire time that the parents are involved in their tasks, without the need for frequent reinforcement (within certain developmental limits of children's attention spans). The parent has to invest the time initially in frequent visits to the child in order to achieve the eventual goal of having the child play independently for sustained periods.

INCREASING PARENTAL MONITORING OF CHILDREN'S ACTIVITIES

Recent research suggests that inadequate parental monitoring of children's behavior and activities is a major contributor not only to noncompliant and aggressive behavior by children toward others, especially peers and siblings, but also to the development of clandestine noncompliant behaviors. Covert antisocial behaviors such as stealing, destruction of property, vandalism, and fire setting, as well as lying to avoid detection, seem to flourish when parents fail to adequately monitor the activities of their typically noncompliant children, both in and out of the home. This monitoring does not mean constant and proximal supervision of every activity of the child but frequent, periodic checking of the child's activities at random intervals when the child is outside the immediate vicinity of the parent.

You should strongly encourage parents to interrupt periodically their own activities, locate the child, and reward the child for appropriate behavior that has been occurring in the absence of the parent. Such monitoring should be relatively frequent and generally unpredictable from the child's perspective. If the child is found to be misbehaving, swift and appropriate punishment is delivered. One of the greatest difficulties in monitoring child behavior is simply remembering to do so at times when the parent is normally preoccupied with other tasks. Parents can train themselves to monitor child activities more frequently through the use of kitchen timers or those on stove or microwave ovens. Set often throughout the day to intervals of varying lengths, these timers can alert parents to stop their activities when the alarm is heard and seek out their children. Watches that have hourly chimes or alarms can also be used for this purpose.

HOMEWORK

The parents are to choose one or two occasions when the child often disrupts their activities and to practice this attending procedure at those times. I have found it useful to concentrate initially on situations in the home rather than in the homes of others or public places while practicing this procedure. Parents may use a telephone call for practicing the method. If so, I encourage parents to have their spouse or a friend call them daily for the sole purpose of practicing this shaping procedure. This allows the parents to interrupt the call frequently to attend to the child's independent play without being too rude or disruptive to the caller. Gradually, parents will be able to use the method with calls from others without using such frequent reinforcement of the child. Parents should record several sentences each day describing their success or problems in practicing the method. Where two parents are in the home, each should choose a different activity for practice. Finally, parents should be reminded to periodically interrupt their ongoing daily activities to check on the child's own independent play, praise it where appropriate, or punish it as needed. Such frequent monitoring is often required in effectively supervising behavior problem children.

When Praise Is Not Enough—
Poker Chips and Points

GOALS

1. To establish a formal system that makes child privileges contingent on child compliance.
2. To increase parental attention to and reinforcement of child compliance and appropriate social conduct.
3. To decrease arbitrariness in parental administration of child privileges.

MATERIALS REQUIRED

- Parent handout
    Home Poker Chip/Point System

STEP OUTLINE

- Review of homework
- The need for special reward programs
- Advantages of a home chip/point system
- Distribute parent handout
- Establishing the token system
    Choosing chips or points
    Making a list of privileges
    Making a list of child target behaviors
    Assigning prices and wages
    Cautions in starting the program
- Parental reactions to the systems

- Continue previously taught methods
- Implement the chip/point system
- Bring the lists of privileges and jobs to next session

In reviewing the previous week's assignment, you will find that a few parents had great success in implementing the skills of attending to children when they are not disrupting parental work. Others will have noted some improvements but remain unimpressed with the method, while still others had no success at all. Encourage the parents not to be disheartened, as in the present session they will acquire a very powerful system of increasing child compliance. In fact, my experience has been that over half of the families will report a near complete remission of the child's problem behaviors during the coming week in response to this program. Others will have dramatic success, but some behavioral problems will remain. It is the rare family that does not report some improvement in child compliance from the present session, provided they took the time to correctly implement the methods.

THE NEED FOR SPECIAL REWARD PROGRAMS

Scientific research is discovering that many clinic-referred children have significant problems with sustained attention, impulsivity, and self-control, which are more likely to be natural characteristics of the child's behavioral and mental abilities, rather than learned misbehavior. These children appear to be less sensitive to social praise and attention. As a result, they do not often show improvements in their behavior merely as a function of increasing parental attention to compliance. More powerful reinforcement programs will prove necessary. This can be related to the earlier discussion in Step 1 about children's temperamental characteristics and developmental abilities. In short, some children will simply not perform at normal levels of compliance for mere social praise and attention; more powerful reinforcement systems must be used. For such children, praise is not enough.

It is helpful to refer back to Step 1 and the idea introduced there that some children are handicapped in their behavioral control. Such children require prosthetic behavior-change methods to permit them to do what other children can do without such formal, artificial, or intense reward programs. Explaining this notion often addresses a concern voiced by many parents: other children do not get such special rewards for doing what they are expected to do, so why should this child? Clearly the answer is that some children *need* such a systematic reward program, where others do not. However, even normal children often improve their behavior under similar poker chip or point system.

Even in cases where otherwise normal children have oppositional or noncompliant behavior as their only problem, these token systems can result in more rapid behavioral improvements than would have been possible with praise serving as the only reinforcer in the program. Furthermore, such token systems may result in bringing child misbehavior well within normal limits, with changes often maintained after the token system is discontinued. As a result, I strongly recommend the use of this method with all children 4 years of age and older who display oppositional or noncompliant behavior.

You should inform parents that many of them already employ an informal, less systematic reward program with their children. Parents often supplement their praise and attention with promises of special privileges, activities, tangible rewards, or allowances for appropriate compliance. The only additional thing you introduce is a method of accounting that allows both the parent and child to know whether a child has in fact earned the promised privilege. Furthermore, adopting a poker chip or point system also allows parents to reinforce child behaviors more quickly, resulting in greater control over child behavior, and to have some system of reward available at all times for use in managing the child.

Explain to parents that the home chip and point systems, or token economies, are very similar to the monetary system on which our society operates, except on a much smaller scale. Rather than using paper money and metal coins, the family will employ poker chips with young children (8 years and younger) and points recorded in a notebook for older children. As in our large social economy, children in this system will be able to earn chips or points for "work" or compliance and exchange their earnings for a variety of rewards.

Experience with this program shows that children 3 years of age or younger do not respond as well, perhaps because they have not yet acquired the ability to comprehend symbolic reinforcers such as chips, points, or money. Further, their number concepts may not be adequately developed to allow appreciation for the units of payment to be used. For whatever reason, we discourage use of this program for children 3 years or younger. Parents can be taught instead to implement reinforcement programs that rely more on direct tangible rewards for the child, such as snacks, favorite drinks, stickers, or small toys, to supplement their use of attention and affection as rewards. For children 4 to 8 years of age, I recommend the use of a poker chip program, which permits the child to see and exchange tangible reinforcers (chips) as part of the program. For 9-year-olds and older, a point system that records in a notebook the number of points earned or spent is more useful and less offensive to the children. Clinical judgment should be used in deciding which reinforcement method to adopt. Some 9-year-olds may do better on a chip program than a point system. Parents can often suggest which program they believe would be more useful for their child.

ADVANTAGES OF THE CHIP/POINT SYSTEM

The therapist should elaborate for the parents the numerous advantages that accrue from use of a token reinforcement program. Briefly, these are

1. Token systems permit parents to manage child behavior by drawing upon rewards more powerful then mere social praise and attention. Hence, greater and more rapid improvements in compliance can often be achieved, beyond what social attention could accomplish.

2. Token systems are highly convenient reward systems. Chips or points can be taken anywhere, dispensed anytime, and used to earn virtually any form of privilege or tangible incentive.

3. Token rewards are likely to retain their value or effectiveness throughout the day across numerous situations. In contrast, children often satiate quickly with food rewards, stickers, or other tangible reinforcers. Because tokens can be exchanged for an almost limitless variety of rewards, their effectiveness as reinforcers is less likely to fluctuate than that of a particular reward.

4. Token systems permit a more organized, systematic, and fair approach to managing children's behavior. The system makes it very clear what children earn for particular behaviors and what number of points or chips is required for access to each privilege or reward. This precludes the arbitrariness often seen in typical parent management approaches where a child may be granted a reward or privilege on the spur of the moment because the parent is in a good mood rather than because the child has earned it. Similarly, it prevents parents from denying earned rewards simply because the child misbehaved once during that day.

5. Token systems result in increased parental attention to appropriate child behavior and compliance. Because parents must dispense the tokens, they must attend and respond more often to child behaviors they might otherwise have overlooked. The children also make parents more aware of their successes or accomplishments so as to earn the tokens.

6. Token systems teach a fundamental concept of society, that privileges and rewards as well as most of the things we desire in life must be earned by the way we behave. This is the work ethic that parents naturally wish to instill in their children: the harder they work and the more they apply themselves to handling responsibilities, the greater will be the rewards they receive.

ESTABLISHING THE HOME POKER CHIP PROGRAM

As noted above, the poker chip program is meant for children generally between the ages of 4 and 8 years. Parents can assist you in deciding whether poker chips or points will be the more effective tokens for their children. The guidelines for setting up the poker chip program are discussed here, while its modification into a point system is discussed in the next section. Parents should be given the handout for this session, and each step should be discussed in detail. The steps to setting up the chip program are

1. Decide what type of chip is to be used. I encourage parents to use the standard plastic poker chip, although some have used bingo chips, checkers, buttons, or other durable, small, yet convenient tokens. In using the colored poker chips, I have found it helpful to take one of each color (white, blue, and red), tape them to a small sheet of cardboard, and display them in a convenient, visible location for easy reference by the child. On each chip, the parent should write the number of chips they represent. The white chip can be worth 1 chip, the blue one 5 chips, and the red one 10 chips. For 4- and

5-year-olds, this need not be done, as each chip, regardless of color, represents only one chip.

2. The parents should take time to explain to the child the program that is about to be implemented. The parents can explain that they would like to provide the child with greater rewards for all of the work the child has been doing about the home. This sets a positive tone in establishing the program, rather than telling the child that, because of misbehavior he or she is now going to have all privileges taken away and will have to earn them back again.

3. The parent and child should construct a container that will serve as the bank for storing the chips earned by the child. Parents can make this fun by decorating a shoe box or large plastic jar with designs prepared by the child.

4. The parent should take time to sit down with the child and construct a list of privileges the child enjoys. Generally, children will suggest special or exceptional privileges that they do not ordinarily have available to them each day, such as going out to eat or to the movies, or buying toys. Parents can list these but should also include those privileges available each day, such as watching television, playing video games or a stereo, riding a bike, or going to a friend's home. The list should contain no less than 10 privileges, while 15 is even better. Approximately one third of these should be short-term rewards that are available to the child every day and for which he or she will have to pay but a small number of chips. These are things like watching television, riding a bike, playing with special toys in the home, going to a neighborhood friend's home, or having a special dessert after dinner. Approximately one third of the privileges should be mid-term ones that will require several days of earnings to purchase. These can be things like staying up past bedtime, watching a special movie or television program not usually shown, spending the night at a friend's home, or helping the parents perform some desirable activity (baking, building things, etc.). At least one third of the rewards should be highly desired, long-term privileges such as buying things at the store, going to the movies or out to eat, taking a special trip, or having a party with friends. These will be more expensive privileges that the child will have to save for, over several days or weeks.

Note: Parents should not charge children for necessities, such as food, clothing, or a bed.

5. Now the parent and child should cooperate in making a list

of jobs, responsibilities, and other behaviors the parents wish to "target" to increase (sharing with a sibling, waiting one's turn to talk at the dinner table, etc.). These can include jobs such as making a bed, cleaning the bedroom, emptying trash cans, doing dishes, setting or clearing dishes for meals, or doing homework. In addition, certain responsibilities such as dressing for school, dressing for bed, and bathing can be placed on the list, if they have been problematic. The parent can also include social behaviors such as not swearing, hitting, lying, or stealing. In order to reinforce a child for not doing something, parents must establish time periods for which they will pay the child for successfully avoiding these undesirable behaviors. For instance, a child who often argues with a parent might be provided three chips for not arguing between breakfast and lunch, another three for not doing so between lunch and dinner, and a final three for the period from dinner to bedtime. I also believe that parents should inform the child that bonus chips will be given for the attitude shown by the child during the performance of these jobs and behaviors. Such bonuses will not be paid every time the child does the job but are discretionary in that the parent can include them for a positive emotional demeanor by the child during performance of the task.

6. The parent should now take the list of jobs and decide how much is to be paid for each. For 4- and 5-year-olds, the range of chips can be between one and five; for older children a larger range can be used. In general, the more difficult and effortful the job or the more problematic the child has been previously in doing it, the more chips the parents will assign to that task.

7. Now the parent needs to decide how much to charge the child for each reward on the list. This can best be done by first adding up how many chips the child is likely to earn in an average day from doing the routine jobs listed. With this figure in mind, parents should assign enough chips to each privilege so that about two thirds of the daily amount earned will be spent on those rewards the child will want each day (television, riding a bike, etc.). This leaves about one third of the chips to be saved each day for spending on the mid-term and long-term privileges on the list. These are just rough guidelines parents may wish to follow. Once the system is implemented, adjustments can be made to make the system more equitable. The more salient and expensive the privilege, the more chips the child will have to spend to earn it. Parents may wish to include money as a

potential reward the child can purchase with the chips. If so, a limit is set as to how many chips can be cashed in each week for money, to prevent the child from using chips to purchase only money. The money would be dispensed like an allowance.

8. The chip system is implemented immediately after these lists are constructed. I have found it helpful for young prereading children to have their mothers construct separate lists for the rewards and jobs and then to draw next to them pictures that represent the job or reward. Parents may wish to skim through magazine ads to find pictures to cut out and paste next to the items on the lists.

ESTABLISHING A HOME POINT SYSTEM

For children who are over 8 years of age, points are used as reinforcers, rather than chips. The parents take a notebook and organize it like a checkbook. Columns in the notebook are marked with date, item, deposit, withdrawal, and current balance. Whenever a child is to be rewarded for compliance, the parent enters the date, a brief notation as to the behavior performed, the amount of points earned, and the new balance. When a child spends points on a reward or activity, the parent notes the type of reward in the item column, enters the amount spent under "withdrawal," and deducts this amount from the balance. The child is never permitted to make entries in the notebook.

The list of privileges is constructed in the same way as described above for a chip program except, of course, that the privileges are appropriate to the age of the child. In all likelihood, the list of jobs constructed will be somewhat larger than in the chip program since the child's greater abilities permit him or her to assist with more household chores than is the case with a younger child.

The number of points assigned to each privilege and each job on the list is determined in much the same way as in the chip system. The harder the job, the more points paid for doing it. The more valuable the rewards, the more points charged for it. The only difference between the chip and point systems is that larger amounts of points are used. I generally use a range of 20 to 200 points to be paid for the various jobs. Similarly, a large range of points is assigned to the list of rewards and privileges.

Otherwise, the point system operates identically to the chip program. Both parents should utilize the system, and both should award points as soon after the occurrence of compliance as possible. The lists of privileges and jobs should be reviewed periodically and changes made to keep it current with the desires of the children and parents.

CAUTIONS IN STARTING THE PROGRAM

Although the token programs are quite easy to implement and administer, there are certain precautions that parents should observe during the first few weeks of the program. These should be explained to the parents before the session is concluded. A major principle parents must follow during the first week is to use the chip program *only for rewarding good behavior.* Unless they are forewarned, parents have a tendency to use the program to punish unacceptable behavior by taking back chips the child has earned. We have found that when parents use the program for penalizing children this first week, children often lose interest in the program before substantial motivation to participate in it can be generated. In subsequent weeks, you will explain how to use the program as a method of punishment, but this should not be permitted during the first week or so the chip system is implemented.

Parents should also be cautioned that children are much more likely to want to participate in the chip system if parents go out of their way during the first week to give away more chips than they might normally. The children should be rewarded for even the simplest of good behaviors to show them how easy it is to earn chips in the program and to enhance their desire to work within its guidelines. Parental stinginess with the chips during this week is greatly counterproductive to developing motivation of the children to cooperate with the procedures.

The parents must also be instructed that the chips are given only after a behavior or job has been performed, never before the job performance on which the chips are contingent. Some children attempt to barter with their parents or otherwise argue for an advance against future payments, especially if they wish to participate in some desirable activity now for which they do not yet have the requisite number of chips. The rule to follow is that if the child does not have the chips, he or she is not allowed access to the reward.

When the chips are administered, the parent should do so with a pleasant tone of voice, taking care to specify exactly what behavior is being rewarded and giving praise or appreciation to the child along with the chips. When chips are exchanged by the child for a reward, the child is to extract them from the bank and pay them to the parent. I discourage parents from making such withdrawals, as we believe the actual motoric act of both spending and depositing the chips in the bank enhances the program's effectiveness.

With children who are likely to steal, parents should be certain that their container of chips is kept out of reach of the children so that pilfering is discouraged. The child is only permitted to touch those chips in the bank.

If both parents are in the home, both should be strongly encouraged to utilize the chips as rewards. There is a tendency for mothers to play the predominant role in this program. While this may at times be justified by one parent's spending greater time with the child than another, the other parent should be encouraged to award chips during time with the child. This enhances consistency of child management procedures between the parents.

The chips can be used to reward virtually any type of appropriate child behavior, even if it is not on the list. Parents should be reminded of this as some are likely to follow the guidelines of the program quite rigidly, thereby missing opportunities to reinforce compliance. Parents can also begin using the chips to reward children for independent play during times when the parent is busy. The method of shaping discussed in Step 4 can be readily augmented with chips in addition to attention as the reinforcers. The chips are to be dispensed immediately upon the occurrence of child compliance. The greater the delay in dispensing the chips, the less control the program will exert over child compliance.

Every several weeks, parents should review the list of rewards with the child to see if new ones should be added or others dropped because they are never requested by the child. In addition, new jobs and responsibilities can be added to the list as parent and child see fit.

I have found it useful for parents to periodically stop their activities, say every 20 to 30 minutes, throughout the day in order to monitor their child's activities to determine if a reward is appropriate at that time. Some parents choose to set an alarm to remind them of this monitoring. In a few cases, we have suggested that parents place small stickers, such as "smiley face" stickers, throughout the home in places where they commonly look, to serve as reminders to observe and reinforce child behaviors. Such places as the faces of clocks, mirrors, the handle of the telephone, and the control panel of the television set can be excellent places to put such sticker cues.

Parents must be patient with this program. Although many children show changes in compliance during the first day the system is implemented, others take several days to a week before the program is sufficiently motivating to increase child compliance. A few oppositional children may even refuse to participate in the procedure, believing that if they stall and withhold participation the parent will give up using the procedure. In such cases, parents are told that the program is to stay in effect regardless of the children's initial reaction to it. The children simply do not get access to the rewards on the list unless they have earned the chips to do so. Some of these children may spend a few days without any privileges or rewards until this principle is fully appreciated. At that point, the children grudgingly begin to cooperate. This is a rare reaction, however, as the vast majority of children find the program to be a quite positive one.

COMMON PARENTAL REACTIONS

Many parents wish to know if siblings, babysitters, or relatives can use the chip or point systems with the children. I generally permit siblings to reward or take away tokens from a child only if they are in their late teenage years and can be trusted by the parents to use the program fairly and in accord with the guidelines described above. The same applies to babysitters. If the same babysitter is commonly used and is a late teenager or young adult, then he or she may use the token system with the child. Again, parental judgment must be exercised to insure that the system is used fairly with the children. I usually discourage relatives from using the token systems unless they are in frequent contact with the children and have major caretaker responsibilities for them, such as serving as babysitters while the mother or father of the child is working.

Many parents believe that token systems constitute bribery of the child. This reflects a misunderstanding of the concept of bribery. Bribery is the offer of an incentive for performance of an illicit, immoral, or illegal act by another person. Clearly, this is not the case within this token system. The system is very similar to the parents' being paid for working outside the home and is simply a fair wage for a fair day's work by the child. Usually, the complaint of bribery actually relates to parental concerns that the child is being rewarded for doing things for which other children are not usually given rewards. As noted earlier, you may have to explain the notion of a behavioral handicap in the child whereby the token system serves as a prosthetic device permitting the child to overcome the handicap. Without the device, the child remains handicapped. With it, the child may perform activities as normal children do without the prosthetic device.

Some parents believe the token system will be too time-consuming for them. Here you may have to confront the parents as to how motivated they are to help in the behavioral recovery of their child. Parents can be reassured that although the program takes a little more time during its initial few weeks of usage, it will eventually become a habit for the parents and of little inconvenience if they will only stay with the program for a while.

Parents often wish to know if other siblings should be placed on the program. This must be a decision made on the basis of each family's circumstances. The parents can discuss it with the siblings for their opinion or may simply decide that all children in the family will be on chip or point systems. Certainly, the greater the number of children in a family, the more burdensome the system becomes for the parents. Often siblings ask to be placed on a similar program, since they see how participation in it leads to a clear knowledge of what is required to earn privileges.

A few parents often ask when and how they can stop the procedure. It is of interest that such parents wish to discuss stopping treatment even before it is implemented. I generally stipulate that the program must remain in effect for 2 months as a minimum period, at which point a session with the family can be held to discuss its gradual fading. However, many families will find that the program dies a natural death, gradually being faded out without any systematic effort to do so. Parents tend to become inconsistent with the method after several months, especially if the child has been behaving quite well. If parents wish to formally remove the program, I suggest that the child be told that the token system will be removed for one or two days to see how well the child behaves without it. The child will still have rewards and privileges, but they will be granted based upon whether or not the work has been done or the child has been compliant with most requests. If the child is able to sustain his or her compliance during this trial period, then the parents can continue to extend the trial period indefinitely. If problems arise, the child can be returned to the program quite quickly.

HOMEWORK

The parents should continue the special playtime periods with the child as well as working on teaching the child not to interrupt them when they are busy, as was taught in Step 4. The major assignment for this session is to implement the token system. Parents are to construct the lists of responsibilities and privileges within a day or two after the session and implement the system. They are to bring these lists to the next session for review by the therapist. If the child is on a point system, his or her bankbook is to be brought to that session.

STEP SIX
Time Out!

1. To introduce the use of fines into the home token system as punishment for noncompliance and unacceptable social conduct.
2. To train parents in the use of an effective time out (isolation) method as punishment for selected child misbehaviors.

- Home Situations Questionnaire
- Parent handout
    Time Out!

- Review of homework
    Make adjustments to the home token system
- Readminister the Home Situations Questionnaire
- Use of the token system for response cost
- Prepare parents for importance of the session
    It is the most difficult week of the program
    It requires the utmost consistency
- Distribute parent handout
- Thoroughly review all steps of the procedure
    How to use time out for noncompliance
    Where should the time out chair be located
    How long should the child remain in the chair

What to do if the child leaves the chair without permission

Ploys the child may use to avoid time out

How to manage physical resistance by the child

- Parental reactions to the procedure
- Restrictions to using time out this week
- Model the procedure for parents
- Parents practice the procedure

HOMEWORK

- Implement response cost
- Use time out for only one or two noncompliant behaviors
- Record use of time out
- Continue previously taught methods

This session begins with a review of the lists from the token system implemented during the previous week. Take time to troubleshoot any problems that may have arisen, make adjustments to the amounts being awarded or charged for various items on the list, deal with any questions the parents and children may have about continued use of the program, and encourage the parents in its continued use. Many parents will report dramatic changes in child behavior as a result of these token systems. Even if parents believe there are no further behavioral problems with the child, they should still be taught the time out procedure. There is certainly an initial honeymoon period with the token system, in my experience, and the parents must be prepared for the occasional return of some noncompliant behavior even if the child is now behaving normally.

At this point, you should readminister the Home Situations Questionnaire to assess changes achieved in child noncompliance since the previous administration (Step 4). You will most likely note a striking reduction in the severity of the ratings in most situations as a result of the use of the home token system.

IMPLEMENTING A RESPONSE COST PROCEDURE

The token system lends itself for use as an effective form of punishment for unacceptable behavior or noncompliance. The parent merely removes a certain number of chips or points as a penalty for not doing a chore or failing to follow a command or rule. Generally, the amount deducted is the same amount that would have been awarded had the child performed the chore. For instance, if a child normally receives five chips for making the bed upon request, then failure to do so means the child must pay the parent five chips from his or her bank. This is in addition to the opportunity the child has just missed to earn five more chips.

Parents may now wish to add a list of undesirable behaviors to the lists already constructed. This list will consist of those frequently occurring, unacceptable behaviors that will now be fined via tokens should they be displayed by the child. Such behaviors as aggression, lying, stealing, arguing, swearing, or other violations of household rules may be placed on this list. The more severe the misbehavior, the greater the penalty assigned.

Parents must be cautioned about a problem that often arises in using tokens in a response cost procedure, what I call a "punishment spiral." This occurs when a parent fines a child for misbehavior, and the child responds with a tantrum, swearing, or destructiveness. These reactions are then fined because they, too, are unacceptable. This further provokes the child's negative reaction, and the child escalates to further verbal abuse of the parent or destructiveness, which leads to further fines under the response cost program, and so on. The net effect is a spiraling of parental punishment entwined with escalating negative reactions by the child to a point where the child has been fined more points than he or she can ever hope to earn and therefore loses all motivation for the program. This dilemma can be managed by the parent following this rule: a child is fined once through the point system, and if a negative reaction ensues, the child is sent to time out (as described below).

PREPARING THE PARENTS FOR USING TIME OUT

It is a major purpose of the session to assist the family in developing a more effective style of disciplining the child for noncompliance and other inappropriate behaviors. In doing so, it is essential that you prepare the family for several things that will take place during the coming homework assignment. First, the parents should be prepared for the fact that this will probably be the most difficult week of the program for them. In many cases when the time out procedure is implemented, children may throw temper tantrums lasting as long as an hour or more, which may prove quite aversive to the family. During these tantrums, the parents may feel as if they should capitulate in order to terminate this unpleasant behavior. Although this parental response would certainly be effective at stopping such children from crying or becoming disruptive, it would merely serve to reinforce the future occurrence of such behavior. Thus, once the time out procedure has been instituted, the parents must see it to its final conclusion without acquiescing to the children's tantrums. Parents should be warned to expect a high rate of negative child reactions when time out is first implemented and that this, in fact, reflects that the method will probably eventually prove effective with that child.

Second, the parents must be prepared to use discipline consistently for the child's noncompliance, even if it may inconvenience them to do so. The parents up to this point have probably been quite inconsistent in the manner in which they have handled the child's misbehavior. Inconsistency is often found between parents, in that one employs a more strict technique than the other, who may in fact become less strict to compensate. Parental inconsistency greatly weakens the effectiveness of this procedure and makes it harder to implement successfully on subsequent occasions.

Third, parents should reduce special family activities to a minimum during the coming week so that parents may devote more time to seeing that the time out method is correctly employed. If special activities cannot be rescheduled (e.g., weddings or visits by out-of-state relatives), then you should postpone teaching the procedure until after the special activities have been completed.

INSTRUCTING THE PARENTS IN THE TIME OUT PROCEDURE

This is one of the most effective methods in this program but must be taught with great care and implemented by the parents in close accord with the explanation you will provide. Give the parents the handout and allow adequate time for them to read it.

Parents are taught that from this point forward, when they give a command to the child, they should be prepared to back it up with consequences for noncompliance. If they are not willing to do so, then the command should not be issued. The consequences are to be implemented immediately, and commands are not to be repeated to the child.

When a command is given, the parent should view the sequence of procedures to be followed as occurring in three stages. I often use the analogy of a stoplight to describe these three stages. The first stage involves the parent giving the command in a neutral but businesslike tone of voice. The command is not to be phrased as a question or favor but as an imperative. The parent should follow all of the guidelines in Step 3 for giving effective commands. Once the command is issued, the parent counts to five to themselves to permit 5 seconds or so to elapse. The counting must not be audible, as we are not training children to comply with countdowns. The issuance of the first command is the green light of the traffic signal—everything is still "go" between the parent and child in that no unpleasant or noncompliant behaviors have yet occurred.

After the 5-second count has elapsed, if the child has not yet begun to comply, the parent then issues a warning. This is the yellow warning light of a traffic signal, to follow our analogy a bit further. Like the traffic signal, the parent's warning is to be distinctive from the first command. The parent is instructed to make direct eye contact, to raise the voice to a much louder level, to adopt a firmer posture and stance, to point a finger at the child, and to present the child with the warning, "If you don't do as I say, then you are going to sit in that chair!" The parent points directly to the vicinity where the time out chair is situated. The entire display by the parent should be so constructed as to convey unequivocally to the child that the parent means what is threatened and will not hesitate to place the child in the chair.

After the warning, the parent again silently counts to five to permit another 5 seconds to elapse. If the child has not begun to comply within this time interval, the parent proclaims to the child, "You did not do as I said, now you are going to the chair!" The parent then takes the child firmly by the upper arm or wrist and escorts the child quickly to the time out chair, placing the child firmly in the seat. The parent then states, loudly, "You stay there until I say you can get up!" This step clearly constitutes the red light in the analogy. At this point, no more than 15 seconds has elapsed since the first command was given. As a result, parents find they are not emotionally out of control, as they might have been had they repeated their commands or warnings a multiple of times without gaining compliance. The punishment is therefore implemented at a time when the parent is best capable of pursuing it in a systematic and businesslike fashion. The therapist should decide how loud, firm, and theatrical the parents' display of the warning is to be for the level of severity of the child's behavioral disorder. Mildly disordered children may not require or deserve as loud a warning or intense a parental display over noncompliance as more severely disordered children.

The child is to be taken immediately to the chair once the second count has occurred. Some children may promise to comply at this point, having seen the parent reaching for them to implement the time out. It is too late for that, and the parents are to implement the time out method despite the child's start at compliance. The time for compliance is now over, and the punishment cannot be avoided. Other children will try to resist the time out by complaining, threatening, or throwing a tantrum. The parent is to escort the child, physically if necessary, to the chair regardless of the child's reaction. In short, nothing the child can do will avoid the punishment from being implemented once the 10-second compliance interval has elapsed.

WHERE SHOULD THE CHAIR BE LOCATED?

As the parent handout suggests, there are several appropriate places for the time out chair. The chair should not be located in a closet, a bathroom, or the child's bedroom. It should be placed in a spot that is convenient for the parent to supervise while the parent continues about the housework. A corner of a foyer, a dining room, or a kitchen, or the middle of a hallway are commonly used places. The chair should be a straight-back chair such as that used in a dinette set and should be placed a sufficient distance from the wall so that the child cannot kick the wall without leaving the chair. There should be nothing within easy reach of the child with which to play. The chair should be left out, visible to the child throughout the day, for at least 2 weeks, as it will serve as a good reminder of what consequence will occur for noncompliance.

HOW LONG SHOULD THE CHILD REMAIN IN TIME OUT?

There are numerous variations of time out from reinforcement, each with its own recommended length of time. Many employ a standard time period, regardless of the age of the child. However, this fails to respect the fact that a child's perception of time varies with his or her developmental level. Young children clearly require less time out before they experience the isolation as unpleasant as compared to older children, who may require a longer interval. In the present method, a length of time is assigned based upon the age of the child. There are essentially three conditions that must be met *in sequence* by the child before the time out is terminated.

1. The child must serve a "minimum sentence" as punishment for the infraction. This is to be 1 to 2 minutes per year of the child's age. A 4-year-old would serve a minimum of 4 minutes in time out, for instance.

2. Once the minimum sentence has elapsed, the child must be quiet for a few moments. The child need not be quiet during the minimum sentence interval, but once that has elapsed, the child must be quiet before the parent will approach the chair. The child may be told this on the first occasion time out is used. The parent would say, "I am not coming back to the chair until you are quiet." It should not be repeated. The child need be quiet for but a minute to meet this second condition. When time out is first used, many children will continue to be vocally disruptive after the minimum sentence has elapsed, and this may continue for several minutes to several hours (in rare cases). If so, the child is to remain in time out until he or she has become quiet, even if it initially extends the time out episode to 1 to 2 hours. Experience has shown that after this initial confrontation over the first time out, the length of time children require in time out diminishes greatly as they learn that becoming quiet quickly lessens the time out interval.

3. Finally, the child must consent to do the original directive. For instance, if the child failed to pick up toys and this resulted in his or her being sent to the time out chair, then the child must agree to pick up the toys. If the behavior that resulted in time out cannot be corrected (e.g., the child hit someone or swore at a parent), then the child must promise not to repeat that behavior. In the future, should the child do so, he or she would be immediately taken to the time out chair without a command or warning being given. If the child should refuse to perform the requested task or refuse to make the promise not to repeat the behavior, then the child is told, "All right, then you stay there until I say you can get up!" At this point, the three conditions are to be repeated: the child serves another minimum sentence, must then be quiet for a few moments, and must consent to do what he or she was told. This sequence repeats itself until the child agrees to do what was asked or to promise not to display the misbehavior again, depending upon the reason time out was implemented.

While the child is in the chair, there is to be no discussion or argument with the child. The parent is to return to the housework or other activity, keeping an eye on the child's behavior while in the chair. Siblings or the other spouse are not to speak with the child.

Once the child has done what was asked, then the parent is to indicate in a neutral tone of voice that he or she likes it when the child listens to the parent. No tokens are to be given at this point for compliance, nor is the parent to make any apology, as some parents tend to do, for having had to punish the child. The parent should then monitor the child's behavior for the next occurrence of appropriate child behavior of importance and reinforce the child for that positive behavior. This is done to keep an appropriate balance between positive reinforcement and punishment within this program as well as to show that the parent does not dislike the child but was punishing him or her for the misbehavior.

There are certain instances where this entire sequence of events would not be followed (i.e., command, warning, time out). These instances are either when a previously stated household rule has been violated or when the parent is assigning a chore that requires an extended time to accomplish. In the first case, the child may have violated a clearly understood rule of the household, such as no hitting, no stealing, no taking food from the kitchen without permission, or no playing with dad's power tools. In such a case, the child would be sent to time out immediately without the rule being repeated or a warning given. I often direct parents to post a list of commonly violated household rules in a visible location (refrigerator door) when starting this program and to tell the child that violation of those rules leads to immediate placement in the time out chair without warning. Where the chore given to the child requires extended time to accomplish (clean your room, do your homework, etc.), the parent is to give both the command and warning at the same time. For example, the child is told to clean his or her bedroom, is given 15 minutes to do so, and is warned that if the room is not clean by then, the child will go to time out. This can all be stated by the parent when the initial request is made. The parent should be told to set the time interval on a kitchen timer so that both parent and child will know when the time has expired, avoiding arguments over whether the time has in fact elapsed.

WHAT IF THE CHILD LEAVES THE CHAIR WITHOUT PERMISSION?

You should review the options that parents have for insuring that a child remains in the chair until the parent states that time out is over. The option that we frequently employ is that the child is spanked twice on the buttocks for leaving the chair without permission. Other options will be discussed, but they are believed to be less effective.

When the child first leaves the chair without permission, the parent is to provide a warning. This warning is provided only once, on the first occasion the child leaves the chair and is never repeated during subsequent uses of time out. The parent returns the child to the chair and states, "If you get out of that chair again, I am going to spank you!" This is said quite loudly as the parent points a finger at the child, again adopting a firm stance and posture. While saying the word "spank," the parents should clap their hands loudly in front of the child for dramatic effect. Thereafter, should the child ever leave the chair again without permission, the parent sits in the chair, places the child over a knee, and delivers two (and only two!) swift spanks with an open hand to the child's buttocks. No objects are to be used to spank the child. The child need not be spanked on the bare buttocks, as we have found that the majority of children find spanking through clothing sufficiently aversive not to warrant it. The child is then returned to the chair and told to stay there until the parent has indicated that they can leave.

Many parents will need to be told what exactly constitutes leaving the chair. There are three things that will be considered as leaving the chair. First, if the child's buttocks leave the flat surface of the seat, it will be considered as leaving the chair without permission. Hence, the child can swivel in the seat, turn about and look around, and fidget but cannot lift his or her buttocks from the chair. Second, rocking the chair so that it moves is treated as leaving the chair.

Third, tipping the chair over is also considered as leaving the chair. All three conditions will result in a warning from the parent or a spanking.

Parents are told that spanking is to be used for no other reason than if the child leaves the chair without permission. This restricts the use of physical disciplining of the child to only one behavior—leaving the chair—as opposed to any behavior with which the parent is sufficiently upset to spank or hit the child. Our experience with this procedure suggests that most children will not require spanking or may require only two or three spankings before learning the contingency and agreeing to stay in the chair. Thereafter, spankings are no longer required when time out is used. However, a few children will remain impervious to the spanking procedure, and so a limit on spanking must be discussed with the parents. The limit that we employ in our clinic is that the child is to be spanked no more than four times during the same incident of time out. At this point, the parent is to use a physical restraint procedure.

There are several forms of restraint the parent may wish to use. The preferred method is the parent standing behind the chair and holding the child's arms behind the back of the chair in a firm yet gentle restraint. Another method involves having the parent kneel beside, slightly behind, and to the right of the child, placing one arm across the child's chest and the other behind the back of the chair while locking hands at the opposite side of the chair. This allows the parent to talk in calming tones, reassuring the child that he or she is not being hurt and will be released once the child agrees to remain in the chair. You can discuss which restraint method is preferable to the parents. Again, it should be noted that the need for multiple spankings or restraint is exceedingly rare, with the vast majority of children learning to remain in the chair during the time out interval. As a result, spanking need never be used in the family again, as the time out method serves as the form of punishment for major infractions of rules.

ALTERNATIVES TO SPANKING

A few parents will not wish to employ the spanking procedure contingent on the child leaving time out, and their wishes should be respected. This, of course, assumes that the parents object to spankings for any misbehavior. If not, then the reasons for this objection deserve exploration. There are several alternatives for the parents who wish not to use the spanking method. First, the parent may send the child to his or her room to serve the time out period. Parents should discuss what they intend to do if the child leaves the room without permission. The room should have few if any play things in it if it is to be used for this purpose. Second, the parent may deduct a certain number of tokens from the child's bank account for every infraction of time out, but there are limits to this procedure as well. A third alternative is to threaten the child with removal of some later privilege (watching television, going to a friend's house later that day, etc.) should the child leave time out prematurely. This may work well for older children, provided the privilege to be removed is an especially salient one for the child. Fourth, the parents may elect to use the physical restraint procedure discussed above in lieu of spanking. Finally, the child's time out interval can be extended an additional five minutes for every time he or she leaves the chair. I do not favor this option. There is a limit to this, of course, before the interval becomes ridiculously long due to numerous infractions of the time out procedure. Also, this may lead to a game of "cat and mouse," which the child may find entertaining, and certainly results in his or her not being isolated from the family or from parental attention.

PLOYS SOME CHILDREN USE TO AVOID OR ESCAPE TIME OUT

There are several common ploys that children have used in attempting to escape or avoid the use of the time out procedure by their parents. Two were already noted above, these being the children's promising to do a task once they see their parents are serious about taking them to the time out chair and the children's refusal to go to time out. In either case, the parental response is the same—the children are taken to time out immediately, using slight physical force if need be to achieve that end. However, once in the chair, these children often make further efforts at escape before the time out interval has been satisfactorily served. Listed below are a few common ploys and how they should be managed.

1. The child asks to go to the bathroom. Virtually all of the children whom I have treated have been fully capable of controlling

their bowel and bladder functions for the short interval of time they are in time out. As a result, parents should be instructed that no child is to be permitted to leave time out to use the bathroom. They may do so once the three conditions for terminating time out have been met, as described above. Many children threaten that they will wet themselves if not permitted to use the bathroom, but in the more than 10 years of using this program, only two children have done so, and in both cases it was obviously an intentional display of opposition and defiance to the parents. In both cases, the children remained in time out until the specified conditions were met. They then had to clean up the area and change their clothing once they had complied with the initial command. If children are permitted to leave the time out area prematurely to use the bathroom, common sense dictates that they will employ this tactic frequently and will likely use the time in the bathroom for play. No doubt they will also be difficult to return to the time out area once released from it.

2. The child claims not to love that parent anymore. While most parents see this statement as the temporary, emotionally laden, and manipulative comment that it is, a few are truly upset that their children might say such things and are apparently so insecure in their relationship with the child that they may capitulate and release the child from time out when such a statement is made. Other parents may not go to that extreme of appeasement but may nonetheless experience great guilt and anxiety while the child is uttering such phrases of hatred. You must prepare the parents for such remarks, discuss in advance how they might feel about hearing them, and then direct them not to react to them in any way while the child is in time out. Reassuring the child of parental affection only provides attention to the child during time out and fosters further arguments and tirades against the parents in future episodes of time out.

3. The child attempts to move the chair or tip it over. As noted above, such activities are construed as having left the chair without permission and will be managed by the use of an initial warning or threat of spanking, followed by spanking if such behavior persists. In cases where parents have chosen not to use the spanking procedure, then the alternative they have selected would be used to respond to these instances of rocking, moving, or tipping over the time out chair.

4. The child threatens to get sick and may vomit. Several chil-

dren treated in our clinic each year use the ploy of illness to gain escape from time out. Some state that they have a sore throat (no doubt from their tantrum) while others complain of headaches or stomachaches. Parents should be taught that the child is merely going through the hierarchy of manipulative behaviors that were found successful on previous occasions to see if they will work in this instance. Parents should ignore such statements, unless there is objective evidence of illness prior to having sent the child to time out (e.g., the child has had a cold or flu that day). Once the child discovers that such complaints no longer elicit parental sympathy and attention, they will not be used in subsequent situations when time out is implemented. However, if attended to by a guilt-ridden parent, they would no doubt be used again by the child in future episodes of time out. I have known of one child who actually threatened to vomit if not released from time out. This was a mildly retarded, conduct problem child who had used such a strategy at school to successfully gain teacher attention and avoid punishment. The parents were instructed to ignore such a threat, and the child actually made good on the warning by sticking his finger down his throat and vomitting. The parents were told to require the child to remain in the time out chair until the three conditions above were met, at which point not only did he have to comply with the initial command but to clean up the mess created in the time out area. Obviously, such reactions from children to time out are extremely rare, but all parents should be instructed in their management should their's prove to be that rare child.

5. The child complains of being tired or hungry. Generally, these complaints arise when time out is implemented at bedtime (usually for failing to prepare for bed when asked) or at mealtimes. Parents are to be told that the child is to be sent to time out, even if it means keeping the child up past bedtime. A few parents wonder if this isn't actually reinforcing to the child, since he or she gets to stay up past bedtime. My experience has been that few children desire to stay up past bedtime to sit alone in a chair in a dull corner of the house while others are in the family room watching television. Usually, children wish to stay up past bedtime to remain in the presence of the family, to play, or to continue watching television. Thus, the children will not enjoy the time out and are not likely to behave at bedtime in such a way as to get sent to time out again. However, the therapist should note to the parents that what makes

time out effective is what the children are missing while being in isolation. Since the children are missing little at bedtime other than sleep, the minimum sentence of time out at bedtime may have to be slightly longer (2 minutes per year of age) to make it effective as punishment.

For children who complain of hunger or are missing a family meal while in time out, parents are told that the children are to simply miss that meal but will be allowed to eat again when the next meal is scheduled. Parents are not to go out of their way to save the children's meal for them or to prepare a special meal once the time out episode has ended. If such were to happen, it is highly likely time out during mealtimes would prove an inadequate form of punishment, as the children are missing little if anything during the time out interval. If the children should end the time out interval while the family is still completing a meal, the children are permitted to return to the table to eat, but additional time for eating is not provided beyond when the rest of the family finishes dinner. At that point, the children's plates would be removed even if they had not yet finished the meal. In short, when children are sent to time out, they miss those activities occurring in the family during that time, and these are not to be made up later by the parents.

6. The child who refuses to leave time out. On occasion, a child may refuse to leave the time out chair once the parent grants permission for the child to leave. Such an instance is a clear bid by the child to continue to control the parent–child interaction. In such cases, the parent is to say that since the child did not do what was asked (leave the chair), he or she must sit there again until the parent says it is time to leave. In this instance, the parent assigns another minimum sentence, awaits the child's becoming quiet, and approaches to see if the child agrees to do what was asked.

USING TIME OUT WITH PHYSICALLY AGGRESSIVE CHILDREN

Each year in our clinic a few children, although young in age and small of size, threaten their parents with violence should the parents try to implement time out with that child. Here, careful clinical judgment is required. Some children with a history of violence against others may well be sufficiently dangerous, even to their parents, that residential treatment is required initially to gain control over such behavioral patterns. However, other children are not so dangerous but still cause their parents some fear, especially their mothers, when they make such threats or in fact adopt a pose that is physically threatening to the parent when time out is to be initiated. In my experience, these have always been threats against the mother, not the father. Should the mother sufficiently fear such a response, I have recommended that the mother use the time out for a behavior problem that occurs when the father is usually at home. Time out is not to be used for any other occasions. In such cases, the child will often cooperate with time out, fearing that the father will join the interaction if need be to insure that time out is implemented. Where these children cooperate with time out by the mother, the mother is to tell the child that the time out period will be reduced somewhat because of his or her cooperation. After several weeks of using the procedure while the father is in the home, the mother is instructed to try it when the father is not home. Presumably, the previous few weeks of cooperation from the child with the time out method will generalize to these instances of father absence. Where this fails, consideration should be given to inpatient treatment of this rare, assaultive child.

COMMON PARENTAL REACTIONS

Most parents will be more than willing to implement these procedures with the child during subsequent weeks. Some parents, however, have concerns about the program or reservations about using it. One common parental reaction is that the parent has tried this type of method before but that it has not worked for them. The therapist can explain that it is quite likely that the earlier version of time out was flawed in several respects. First, it is likely that the parents did not implement the program until they were quite angry and frustrated with the child and had repeated their commands many times in order to get the child to comply. This is hardly effective, as time out was used infrequently, not immediately upon the occurrence of the noncompliance, and when the parent was most likely to use an excessive time out period out of anger.

Second, most parents have used time out in a manner that has allowed control of the interval to remain in the hands of the child.

That is, they have told the child to go to his or her room and stay there until he or she was ready to come out and behave properly. This obviously leaves the determination of when to end time out to the child.

A third frequent mistake is that parents have used a standard time out interval, say 5 minutes, for every episode of child misbehavior, regardless of the severity of the infraction or the age of the child. The problem here is that for older children the time out period is too short to be aversive and hence will be ineffective. Furthermore, the time out procedure should be adjusted to fit the severity of the rule violation. That is why this program recommends a range of 1 to 2 minutes for each year of the child's age. Modest rule infractions will receive the smaller amount of time out, while serious infractions will receive the larger amount.

A fourth mistake is using the child's bedroom for time out. While parents may eventually have to do so if they do not wish to spank the child for leaving the time out chair, we recommend that parents not use the child's bedroom initially. The room often has too many objects for play and entertainment, thus diminishing the effectiveness of the time out procedure. If a parent must use the child's room for the time out, then the child's toys and other sources of entertainment should have been removed from the room previous to implementing the procedure. In such cases, parents must decide how they will deal with the child who tries to leave the room without permission.

Finally, it is likely that most parents did not use the time out consistently for misbehavior, thus detracting from its effectiveness. Often the parents used time out only when they were emotionally upset, while not using it for the same rule infraction at other times. Similarly, the parents may have allowed the child to barter a way out of time out by agreeing to comply with the command once it was clear that the parent was about to take the child to a time out location. The present program dictates that once the parent starts to implement time out, it is to be carried through no matter what the child promises to do for the parent at that moment.

Some parents may object to the spanking procedure. When this occurs, the alternatives to spanking can be discussed with the parents. In my experience, fewer than five percent of parents object to using the spanking procedure. Many parents initially expect the average child will require multiple spankings before remaining in the chair. Our experience, however, is that the vast majority of children exposed to the sequence of events in this procedure do not elect to leave the chair without permission or may try to do so once. Some will require one or two spankings beyond the initial warning before learning to remain in time out until the parent grants permission to leave. The very few children where multiple spankings might be required are to be managed using the physical restraint methods described above or sent to their rooms to serve the time out interval.

Many parents inquire as to how they should use the procedure if there are visitors in the home. Their concern here appears to be one of fear of embarrassing the child or themselves. The parents should be told to implement the procedure regardless of the visitors. While apologies may have to be made to the visitors for doing so, this should not preclude the use of the time out procedure. Failure to implement time out in such cases would teach the child that occasions when visitors are in the home are ones in which the child can misbehave with immunity. If the visitors are neighborhood friends of the child, they should be asked to leave once time out has had to be implemented.

RESTRICTIONS ON USING TIME OUT DURING THE FIRST WEEK

If parents were initially to use the time out procedure for all instances of noncompliance, many behavior disorderd children would spend the majority of their day in the chair in a corner. To avoid this excessive disciplining of the child, parents are told that they may use time out for only one or two noncompliant behaviors during the coming week, and these are to be ones occurring only in the home, not in public. We also suggest that the parents wait for a week before tackling bedtime problems. This allows the child to become accustomed to the time out procedure and for its effects perhaps to generalize to commands given at bedtime so that parents may not actually have to use the procedure at bedtime. They may wish to choose particular commands that are problematic for the child, such as picking up toys, getting dressed for school, or doing homework.

Others will choose household rules that are frequently violated, such as hitting, swearing, or lying. In either case, only two commands or rules are to be chosen for use with the time out method.

The restriction against using the method in public places for the time being is founded on the belief that the time out procedure requires slight modification to be effective in public places, as well as the fact that parents must be prepared for possible reactions they may get from others who witness their use of time out with a child. In addition, by introducing the procedure at home for several weeks, the possibility develops that improvement in the home will generalize to commands given in public places. In other words, once the children realize the parents mean business and have used the time out method when it was threatened, they may learn not to disobey commands or warnings issued in public places.

Parents should also be told that, should they encounter problems with the procedure, they should call you immediately. Clinicians using this program should routinely give parents their home and work telephone numbers for use during this week should problems arise. It is extremely rare that any parents will call, but the security of knowing the therapist is readily available and the feelings of importance this lends to the procedure are quite therapeutic.

Parents will often ask what they should do to manage misbehaviors that are not to be the objects of time out this week. They should be reminded of the availability of the response cost method (fining tokens for misbehavior), which can be used with any behavior problem. In some instances, parents may choose to use both methods of punishment for especially serious rule infractions. In this case, the child would be fined tokens from his or her bank account as well as sent to the time out chair for a longer-than-usual minimum sentence.

MODELING THE PROCEDURES FOR PARENTS

Throughout the discussion of the procedures, you can role-play the methods with a pretend child or may in fact have one of the parents pretend to be a child for the sake of demonstrating the sequence of events. If an individual family is undergoing the training and the child is present, you may role-play the method with the child, being certain to explain to the child that it is only pretend for now and that he or she will not be spanked. The parent is then to role-play the method with you serving as the pretend child. Forehand and McMahon (1981) suggest that the parent never serve as the child during role-play in front of the child, as it may teach the child that the parent can be punished or placed in time out.

The parent and child can then go to a playroom together where the parent issues a variety of commands to the child until one is disobeyed. At this point the parent implements time out so that you can evaluate how well it is being used by the parent. In the case of older children who have heard you explain the method, such children usually will not violate parental commands in the playroom as they realize what the consequences will be. In such cases, role-playing the procedure will have to suffice. Role-playing is also the mode of parental practice when this procedure is taught as part of a group parent training class. At first, you should choose a parent to serve as the pretend child for the role-play demonstration. Then the parents pair off and practice with other parents, taking turns in practicing the parental role in the procedure under your supervision. Whether in individual or group training, you should require the parents to role-play the spanking procedure using your forearm placed across the lap of the parent and spanked. This permits you to gauge the force of the parent's spank and make adjustments in it accordingly.

HOMEWORK

Parents will of course continue to use the previously taught procedures. I often find at this step that parents are beginning to discontinue the special playtimes. They should be encouraged to keep these activities going, particularly this week, as they will serve to offset the deleterious effects of the punishment program on the parent–child relationship.

Besides implementing the time out procedure, parents are to record in a diary every instance when time out was employed, what the child did to receive time out, and how well the parents felt the procedure was implemented. Parents should also record the length of each time out episode. Before leaving the session, parents are to stipulate to the therapist the two noncompliant behaviors with which they will employ time out this week as well as the location in the home where the time out is to be served.

STEP SEVEN

Extending Time Out
to Other Misbehaviors

GOALS

1. To troubleshoot and resolve problems parents are encountering in using the time out method with the child.
2. Where appropriate, to extend the use of the time out method to other commands or rules that elicit noncompliance.

MATERIALS REQUIRED
- No handouts

STEP OUTLINE
- Review homework records on time out
- Select two or more additional noncompliant behaviors for use with time out

HOMEWORK
- Continue using and recording time out method

The session begins with the usual review of parent homework records and discussion of problems the parents may have had in implementing the time out method. The majority of this session is spent in reviewing the instances in which time out was used, how the parents felt about it, problems that may have been encountered in its implementation, and any minor adjustments that may have to be made to the parent's use of the procedures. No new material is introduced in this session. For some families, the session will be brief as they have been successfully using the procedure since the past session. For others, the session may involve a lengthy discussion of problems the parents have experienced and how they should resolve them in their use of time out.

With most parents, the session will conclude with a discussion of the two or three new noncompliant behaviors with which the parents are to use time out in the next week. The parents are to continue keeping records of their use of time out. For a few families, there will be no further significantly noncompliant behaviors of the child that warrant attention. In this case, parents are told to use the time out procedure with whatever behaviors they wish whenever it seems appropriate to do so. No record keeping need be done for these families. There will be a few families who have met such striking problems in using time out at home that you may wish to have the parent and child practice the methods once again in the clinic before allowing the procedure to be used at home. This often reveals the problems the parents may be having in trying to use time out with the child. In any case, you should insure that the parents adequately grasp the essential elements of successfully using the procedure before permitting them to extend its use to additional child behavior problems.

STEP EIGHT

Managing Noncompliance in Public Places

GOALS

1. To train parents in adapting the previously taught child management methods for use in public places.
2. To teach parents a three-step "think aloud–think ahead" procedure for reducing public misbehavior in children.

MATERIALS REQUIRED

- Home Situations Questionnaire
- Parent handout
  Managing Children in Public Places

STEP OUTLINE

- Review of homework
- Readminister Home Situations Questionnaire
- Anticipating problem behavior—the key to success
- Distribute parent handout
- Review important details of handout
  Setting up rules before entering public places
  Establishing an incentive for compliance
  Establishing a disciplinary response for noncompliance
  Monitoring, attending to, and rewarding compliance in the public place
- Types of places in which methods can be used
- Parental reactions to the methods

- Make two bogus shopping trips for practice
- Record information concerning these trips

Review the homework and resolve any minor problems the parents may still be having in their use of the time out procedure. Then readminister the Home Situations Questionnaire to assess the degree of improvement in child compliance to date as a result of treatment. Significant change should be evident in these ratings as compared to those taken in the initial evaluation of the child prior to training. Introduce the new material for this session by discussing the kinds of problems the parents are facing in managing their behavior problem child in public. After a detailed review of these problems, the therapist introduces the notion that most parents do not think ahead about the kinds of problems they may face with a child in public places. Instead, many enter public places such as stores without a thought as to how they will cope with a behavior problem from the child should it arise. Only when the noncompliance or behavior problems occur does the parent begin to think about how to deal with it. This is probably the worst time to begin planning a strategy for managing the problem, as the child will certainly be disruptive and the parent is likely to be angry and anxious because of others watching this scene. All of these factors will detract from developing a reasonable and effective method of dealing with the problem.

As a result, anticipating behavioral problems is a key concept in learning to manage children effectively in public places. Many parents have sufficient experience to know what types of public places are likely to evoke noncompliant behaviors and what type of behavioral problem is likely to arise. If parents would therefore take a few moments before entering such places in order to develop a plan to use should noncompliance occur and to make this plan clear to the child, a large amount of child misbehavior in public places could be avoided. In those cases where problems were not avoided, at least the parent would have established a quick and effective reaction to managing the misbehavior long before it attracts the attention of others in that setting.

Emphasis needs to be given to the concept of anticipation and planning in coping with the misbehavior of children in public places.

DISTRIBUTE AND REVIEW PARENT HANDOUT

The handout for this session is brief, quite clear, and easily implemented by most parents. You should review it step-by-step, in as much detail and with as many examples as are necessary to illustrate the procedure. Essentially, the methods are no different than those previously taught but with some minor modifications because no time out chair is readily available in public places. The critical feature to this handout is the concept stressed at the beginning of the session—thinking ahead and developing a strategy of child management.

There are three elementary steps to this method, and they involve teaching parents to:

1. Stop before entering any public place and establish the rules that the child is expected to follow in that place. At first, the parent is to stop just in front of the entrance to the public place. Then the parent is to establish three or four rules that the child is to follow in the place but which the child has previously had trouble obeying. The child is to repeat these rules verbatim before proceeding to the next step. For instance, before entering a store with a young child, the parent may say that the rules are "Stand close, don't touch, and don't beg!" The child is then to repeat these rules to the parent. On subsequent trips to stores, the parent need only prompt the child to repeat the rules by saying, "What are the rules?" If the child fails to recall them properly, the parent restates them and has the child repeat them again. For older children, these rules might be "Stay next to me, don't touch anything, and do as I say!" Other rules more appropriate to restaurants, churches, or the homes of others would be substituted for those situations.

2. Establish an incentive for compliance. For children who are already on the poker chip or point systems, these can be used quite readily to reinforce compliance with the rules established in paragraph 1 above. The parent can merely tell the child that he or she will earn a certain number of points or chips for obeying the rules while in the public place. For very young children not on a token system, the parent can take a small cellophane bag of snack treats to the store for use with the child. The chance to earn them would be explained to the child before entering the store. A few parents may wish to promise the child a reward that will be purchased at the end of the trip. If this is done, it should be used sparingly or the child will expect that every trip to a public place results in such purchases. Whichever method of incentive is employed, it is explained to the child before entering the public place.

3. Establish a disciplinary response for noncompliance. The parents review with the child what form of punishment they will employ if the child breaks any of the rules just stated or other rules previously explained to be operative in that public place. Wherever possible, the punishment should be the use of the time out procedure used at home or the removal of tokens, depending upon the severity of the rule infraction and whether the child is already on a token system at home. Since no chairs are readily available for time out in public places, parents should be prepared to quickly locate a dull corner of the public place where the child would serve the time out period should misbehavior develop. This can be easily accomplished, as most parents know the arrangement of the stores, restaurants, churches, and other public places that they frequently visit. Again, whichever method is to be used, it is to be clearly explained to the child before entering the public place.

Upon entering the building, the parent is to scan the area quickly for a potential time out corner and then begin to do whatever was planned. Periodically throughout the trip, the parent should attend to and praise the child for adhering to the rules of the setting. For children on token systems, parents can periodically dispense chips or points to the child throughout the time they remain in the public place. It is crucial that parents not wait until the end of the trip before commenting about the child's performance but that they attend to the child's compliance throughout the trip, providing periodic feedback to the child.

If the parent must implement time out, the child is immediately taken to a quiet, out-of-the-way corner of the building and told to stand in the corner facing the wall until the parent says the child can leave. At this point, the procedure to be followed is exactly like that used at home except that the minimum sentence needs to be only a half minute or so for each year of the child's chronological age. We have found that shorter intervals of time out are just as effective in public places as are longer intervals at home. This is probably because the child is missing a great deal of interesting activities while in time out in public places and most children experience embarrassment at being timed out in such places, which further contributes to its aversiveness and hence its effectiveness.

The parent is to remain near the child during time out but should be busy with some other activity so as not to provide attention to the child during this procedure. As at home, the time out episode ends when the child has (1) served a minimum sentence, (2) become quiet for a few moments, and (3) agreed to comply with the rule that was just violated. If the child leaves time out prematurely, the child is returned to the corner and warned that if time out is interrupted again, he or she will be spanked. Rarely do children continue "testing" this situation, but should they leave time out again without permission, the parent would deliver one swift spank to the child's buttocks before returning the child to the time out corner.

Because time out has worked successfully at home for the previous few weeks, when it is threatened for use in public places children come to expect that the parent will indeed implement the procedure and rarely challenge the parental authority in such public places. When the child does violate the explicit rules set forth, the parent should implement the time out very quickly and without warning, since the child was already warned before entering the public place. I have found that when children are taught that such parental reactions will be swift and decisive, they rarely violate these rules in public places. For parents who prefer not to spank the child, alternatives should be discussed. These can be relying on fines in the token system, removing the child from the store, or threatening to remove a privilege the child might have later in the day.

There will be some places in which time out in the building may not be possible, as in grocery stores where few, if any, dull corners exist. In such cases, the parents can implement one of these alternatives. First, determine if the child can be taken swiftly out of the building and placed against a wall to serve the time out there. If not, a second option is to take the child to the car and have the child sit on the floor of the back seat of the car. The parent remains in the front seat or standing outside next to the car. A third alternative is for the parent to record the child's misbehavior in a notebook carried by the parent for this explicit purpose. Usually, a small pocket spiral notepad serves this purpose well. If this option is to be used, it should be explained to the child in front of the public place. Basically, the method involves having the parent record the incident in the notebook, and immediately upon the family's return home, the child is to serve a minimum sentence for each infraction of rules recorded in the notebook. I have discovered that keeping a picture of the child in the notebook that shows the child sitting in the time out chair at home is a useful device for refreshing the child's memory of time out at home. The picture is shown to the child during the explanation of this method before the parent and child enter the public place. A fourth alternative is to place a hash mark with an ink pen on the back of the child's hand for each rule violation in the store. Like the notebook, this method requires that the child serve a minimum sentence in time out for each rule violation so recorded, immediately upon the family's return home from that trip.

REVIEW USE OF PROCEDURE IN
VARIOUS PUBLIC PLACES

You can now select several public places in which the child misbehaves and review with the parents how the three steps above would be used before entering those places. The parents should discuss what rules they would establish for those places in which the child commonly misbehaves. In addition, the parents can discuss what forms of incentives or discipline they might wish to use in those places. You can illustrate the use of the method for a store, a restaurant, a church, and the home of someone they are visiting. The method can also be used prior to setting out on long car trips. In addition to following these steps, parents should also take along various play activities to occupy the children during the lengthy car trip so as to preclude misbehavior developing from boredom during the trip. In case the children should misbehave, points or chips can be deducted during the trip. To use time out the parent parks the car in a safe place alongside the roadway and has the child sit on the floor of the back seat for the time out interval. Time out should not be implemented while the parent is trying to drive the vehicle.

MANAGING PARENTAL EMBARRASSMENT

As in previous sessions, you should discuss the parents' reactions to the use of this method. One reaction that can greatly impede the effective use of this program in public places is the embarrassment parents believe they will suffer should they implement the method while others are watching them. For most parents, the following simple explanation will suffice. Little if any behavior problem is likely to develop if the parent follows the three steps discussed above before entering the public place. The odds of a problem developing are further reduced by the parents' use of ongoing attention, praise, and rewards for child compliance in the public place. Even where misbehavior develops, it will often be at a much reduced level of disruption because the parent will respond to it swiftly and decisively before it gets out of hand. All of these are likely to reduce any opportunity for the parent to experience embarrassment from this program.

There are always a few parents, however, who are overwhelmed with the prospect of such embarrassment, so that they cannot use the methods described above very effectively. For such parents, you may wish to spend a few sessions at this point utilizing a rational-emotive approach to coping with such parental feelings. Two books that I have found useful for parents to review in such cases are *Your Erroneous Zones* by Wayne Dyers and *A New Guide to Rational Living* by Albert Ellis and Robert Harper. A short review of rational-emotive therapy methods is available in the book by James Bard entitled *Rational–Emotive Therapy in Practice*, particularly chapter 5 on parent–child interactions.

In essence, this approach stresses that maladaptive or unpleasant parental emotions in such circumstances are the result of negative and often overly critical self-statements and self-evaluations that the parent is making during the interaction with the child. Parents are taught to identify these negative and maladaptive statements and to substitute positive coping self-statements in such situations. Sometimes, parents may need to record their thoughts in a public place should they experience serious emotional upset over having to deal with their child's behavior. These notes can then by reviewed as part of therapy, and positive coping statements can be designed by the therapist for use by the parent in subsequent encounters with the child's misbehavior in public.

HOMEWORK

Parents are to continue all of the methods previously taught in this program. During the next week, the parents are to make two bogus trips to stores or other public places, with the sole intent of practicing the steps discussed above. Parents may wish to record information about these trips for review by the therapist at the next session.

STEP NINE

Handling Future
Behavior Problems

GOALS

1. To encourage parents to think about possible future behavior problems and how they could use the methods of this program to address the problems.
2. To prepare parents for the termination of therapy if no other types of treatment are to be used with this family.

MATERIALS REQUIRED

- Parent handout
    Managing Future Behavior Problems

STEP OUTLINE

- Review of homework
- "Think aloud–think ahead" method for in-home misbehavior
- Distribute parent handout
- Review steps in parent handout
    Keep records of problem behaviors
    Review these records for parental mistakes
    Correct management errors where necessary
    Develop an incentive system
    Design a disciplinary method
    Implement the new program
    Evaluate program effectiveness

HOMEWORK

- No homework

You should review the attempts of the parents during the previous week in coping with misbehavior in public places. Assuming this has gone well for the family, you can now explain that these same steps could be followed for problems within the home as well. There are many instances where it is predictable that a behavior disordered child may display inappropriate behavior, such as when visitors are in the home, when certain friends of the child come to play, or when a party at home is about to begin. Parents can very easily review the three steps taught in the previous session before these events are about to occur in the home. By doing so, parents will find that such anticipation and planning greatly decreases the likelihood that misbehavior will occur. Examples of using these three "think aloud-think ahead" steps in the home can be provided by you for review with the family. Although this is usually the last session of the program, some therapists may wish to assign as homework the implementation of the three steps for an in-home misbehavior, the use of which would then be reviewed during a subsequent session. In other words, this need not be the concluding session of parent training should the therapist believe that further rehearsal and implementation of the methods of the program is required by a particular family.

DISTRIBUTE AND REVIEW PARENT HANDOUT

The parent handout is quite self-explanatory and will receive little comment here. Basically, it reviews the procedures that parents have been following throughout the course of training and how these might be applied should the child develop a new misbehavior. The handout explains that parents are to begin keeping a record of the misbehavior and to review that record after 7 to 10 days to see if it reveals common mistakes the parents may have returned to, now that parent training is completed. This is followed by the parents' correcting any mistakes they have detected. If this fails to improve the behavior, then the parent is to establish both an incentive and disciplinary program for the particular behavior problem. Usually this involves using privileges or a token system as rewards and response cost or time out as the punishment. Parents are to continue keeping a record of the problem behavior throughout this time. If the misbehavior still fails to decline, they should schedule another appointment with you, being sure to bring along their notes for your review.

CHALLENGING PARENTS WITH HYPOTHETICAL BEHAVIOR PROBLEMS

One of the major goals of this session is to begin weaning the parents' dependence upon you as the individual who is to solve the child's behavior problems. The parents now have all the skills necessary to cope with the vast majority of behavior problems displayed by most children. Their task now is to begin thinking how they might use these skills in managing any future misbehavior that might arise. You can pose a hypothetical behavior problem for the family and request them to think about how they would approach its treatment using the skills and methods they have acquired in the training program. Your assistance can be given where necessary but should be sparing. Instead, questioning the parents in a Socratic style may help lead them to the correct use of a procedure while fostering their independence from you.

HOMEWORK

There is generally no homework for this session, although you may wish to assign as homework the use of the "think aloud–think ahead" steps for an in-home child behavior problem. This would be reviewed with the parents in a subsequent session, perhaps the booster session discussed below.

STEP TEN

Booster Sessions

At the conclusion of Step 9, you should schedule a 1-month booster session. This meeting will be used to review some of the general principles taught in the program and any methods about which the parents have questions, and to see how well the family continues to implement the procedures of the program. At this point, the parents would complete the posttreatment questionnaires and rating scales. The parent and child could be scheduled for an observational assessment of their interactions either in the home or in a clinic observation room using the direct observation techniques described in Part 1. Some therapists find it helpful to schedule a second booster session 3 to 6 months after this for further monitoring of the family's progress with the procedures. Throughout these follow-up intervals, the family can be encouraged to call you for assistance should it be required.

3

Assessment Materials
and Parent Handouts

PARENT-CHILD INTERACTION INTERVIEW FORM

Child's name _____ Date _____
Parent's name _____
Interviewer _____

Instructions: The interviewer should question the parents concerning each area or home situation listed below. Should the parent state that an interaction problem exists in that setting, the interviewer should follow up with the following seven questions:

1. What exactly does the child do in this setting?
2. What is your response to the child's misbehavior?
3. What does your child do in response to this?
4. How does the interaction finally end?
5. How often does this problem occur? Daily? Weekly?
6. How do you feel about this misbehavior?
7. On a scale of 1 to 9 where 1 represents no problem and 9 represents a severe problem, how would you rate this problem?

INTERVIEW QUESTIONS

1. In general, how would you say you and your child get along with each other each day?

        rating _____

2. Play
    How well do you and your child get along when your child is in the house alone and you are around?

        rating _____

Adapted from C. Hanf, University of Oregon Health Sciences Center, 1976.

How does it go when there are other children around?

rating _____

3. Eating and Mealtimes

Let's turn to a specific part of the day—mealtimes. How does your child manage him- or herself at that time? It's not what they eat, but the child's behavior that's important here.

rating _____

4. Dressing and Handling Clothes

What is dressing and undressing time like with your child?

rating _____

5. Washing and Bathing

What is washing and bathing time like with your child?

rating _____

6. Use of the Telephone

Suppose the telephone rings for you and your child is in the house, how do things go?

rating _____

7. Television Watching

Television watching often produces problems for the family. What is it like in your family when your child is near the set and others are watching?

rating _____

8. Visitors in Your Home
   Do you tend to have visitors in your home?
   How frequently?   Rarely _____   Moderate _____   Often _____
   How does this go with your child when you do?

        rating _____

9. Visiting Others' Homes
   Now, let's look at the other side of the coin: . . . what is it like
when you take your child to visit other homes? How does that go?

        rating _____

10. Public Places
    Supermarkets, restaurants, and stores all seem to be built for
giving trouble to parents. Do you have any trouble with your child
in such places?

        rating _____

11. Mother Occupied in the Home
    Suppose you are busy about the house doing what needs to
get done. What is your child like when you are busy?

        rating _____

12. When Father Is Home
    Does your child have any behavior problems when his or her
dad is at home?

        rating _____

13. Chores
Is your home one in which children have chores to do? If so, how does your child respond when given chores to do?

rating _____

14. Homework
Does your child attend school? If he or she is given homework to do, how does that go?

rating _____

15. Bedtime
Does your child have behavior problems when he or she is told to go to bed?

rating _____

16. Other Situations
Are there any other situations in which your child has problems with his or her behavior?

rating _____

Total number of problem settings _____
Mean severity score __ (sum of all ratings divided by number of ratings)

HOME SITUATIONS QUESTIONNAIRE

Child's name _____ Date _____

Name of person completing this form _____

Instructions: Does your child present any problems with compliance to instructions, commands, or rules for you in any of these situations? If so, please circle the word yes and then circle a number beside that situation that describes how severe the problem is for you. If your child is not a problem in a situation, circle No and go on to the next situation on the form.

Situations	Yes/No		If yes, how severe?	
	(Circle one)	Mild	(Circle one)	Severe
Playing alone	Yes	No	1 2 3 4 5 6 7 8 9	
Playing with other children	Yes	No	1 2 3 4 5 6 7 8 9	
Mealtimes	Yes	No	1 2 3 4 5 6 7 8 9	
Getting dressed/undressed	Yes	No	1 2 3 4 5 6 7 8 9	
Washing and bathing	Yes	No	1 2 3 4 5 6 7 8 9	
When you are on the telephone	Yes	No	1 2 3 4 5 6 7 8 9	
Watching television	Yes	No	1 2 3 4 5 6 7 8 9	
When visitors are in your home	Yes	No	1 2 3 4 5 6 7 8 9	
When you are visiting some-one's home	Yes	No	1 2 3 4 5 6 7 8 9	
In public places (restau-rants, stores, church, etc.)	Yes	No	1 2 3 4 5 6 7 8 9	
When father is home	Yes	No	1 2 3 4 5 6 7 8 9	
When asked to do chores	Yes	No	1 2 3 4 5 6 7 8 9	
When asked to do home-work	Yes	No	1 2 3 4 5 6 7 8 9	
At bedtime	Yes	No	1 2 3 4 5 6 7 8 9	
While in the car	Yes	No	1 2 3 4 5 6 7 8 9	
When with a babysitter	Yes	No	1 2 3 4 5 6 7 8 9	

.... For Office Use Only ....

Total number of problem settings _____ Mean severity score _____

CHILDREN'S HOSPITAL NATIONAL MEDICAL CENTER
Washington, D. C. 20010

Parent's Questionnaire

Name of Child _____ Date _____

Please answer all questions. Beside *each* item below, indicate the degree of the problem by a check mark (✓)

	Not at all	Just a little	Pretty much	Very much
1. Picks at things (nails, fingers, hair, clothing).				
2. Sassy to grown-ups.				
3. Problems with making or keeping friends.				
4. Excitable, impulsive.				
5. Wants to run things.				
6. Sucks or chews (thumb; clothing; blankets).				
7. Cries easily or often.				
8. Carries a chip on his shoulder.				
9. Daydreams.				
10. Difficulty in learning.				
11. Restless in the "squirmy" sense.				
12. Fearful (of new situations; new people or places; going to school).				
13. Restless, always up and on the go.				
14. Destructive.				
15. Tells lies or stories that aren't true.				
16. Shy.				
17. Gets into more trouble than others same age.				
18. Speaks differently from others same age (baby talk; stuttering; hard to understand).				
19. Denies mistakes or blames others.				
20. Quarrelsome.				
21. Pouts and sulks.				
22. Steals.				
23. Disobedient or obeys but resentfully.				
24. Worries more than others (about being alone; illness or death).				

25.	Fails to finish things.				
26.	Feelings easily hurt.				
27.	Bullies others.				
28.	Unable to stop a repetitive activity.				
29.	Cruel.				
30.	Childish or immature (wants help he shouldn't need; clings; needs constant reassurance).				
31.	Distractibility or attention span a problem.				
32.	Headaches.				
33.	Mood changes quickly and drastically.				
34.	Doesn't like or doesn't follow rules or restrictions.				
35.	Fights constantly.				
36.	Doesn't get along well with brothers or sisters.				
37.	Easily frustrated in efforts.				
38.	Disturbs other children.				
39.	Basically an unhappy child.				
40.	Problems with eating (poor appetite; up between bites).				
41.	Stomach aches.				
42.	Problems with sleep (can't fall asleep; up too early; up in the night).				
43.	Other aches and pains.				
44.	Vomiting or nausea.				
45.	Feels cheated in family circle.				
46.	Boasts and brags.				
47.	Lets self be pushed around.				
48.	Bowel problems (frequently loose; irregular habits; constipation).				

Note. Reprinted by persmission of C. K. Conners.

CHILDREN'S HOSPITAL NATIONAL MEDICAL CENTER
111 Michigan Avenue, N. W.
Washington, D. C. 20010

Teacher's Questionnaire

Name of Child _____

Date of Evaluation _____

Grade _____

Please answer all questions. Beside *each* item, indicate the degree
of the problem by a check mark (✔)

	Not at all	Just a little	Pretty much	Very much
1. Restless in the "squirmy" sense.				
2. Makes inappropriate noises when he shouldn't.				
3. Demands must be met immediately.				
4. Acts "smart" (impudent or sassy).				
5. Temper outbursts and unpredictable behavior.				
6. Overly sensitive to criticism.				
7. Distractibility or attention span a problem.				
8. Disturbs other children.				
9. Daydreams.				
10. Pouts and sulks.				
11. Mood changes quickly and drastically.				
12. Quarrelsome.				
13. Submissive attitude toward authority.				
14. Restless, always "up and on the go."				

15.	Excitable, impulsive.			
16.	Excessive demands for teacher's attention.			
17.	Appears to be unaccepted by group.			
18.	Appears to be easily led by other children.			
19.	No sense of fair play.			
20.	Appears to lack leadership.			
21.	Fails to finish things that he starts.			

22.	Childish and immature.			
23.	Denies mistakes or blames others.			
24.	Does not get along well with other children.			
25.	Uncooperative with classmates.			
26.	Easily frustrated in efforts.			
27.	Uncooperative with teacher.			
28.	Difficulty in learning.			

Note. Reprinted by permission of C. K. Conners.

151

SCHOOL SITUATIONS QUESTIONNAIRE

Child's name _____ Date _____

Name of person completing this form _____

Does this child present any behavior problems for you in any of these situations? If so, indicate how severe they are.

Situations	Yes/No (Circle one)		If yes, how severe? Mild (Circle one) Severe
While arriving at school	Yes	No	1 2 3 4 5 6 7 8 9
During individual desk work	Yes	No	1 2 3 4 5 6 7 8 9
During small group activities	Yes	No	1 2 3 4 5 6 7 8 9
During free playtime in class	Yes	No	1 2 3 4 5 6 7 8 9
During lectures to the class	Yes	No	1 2 3 4 5 6 7 8 9
At recess	Yes	No	1 2 3 4 5 6 7 8 9
At lunch	Yes	No	1 2 3 4 5 6 7 8 9
In the hallways	Yes	No	1 2 3 4 5 6 7 8 9
In the bathroom	Yes	No	1 2 3 4 5 6 7 8 9
On field trips	Yes	No	1 2 3 4 5 6 7 8 9
During special assemblies	Yes	No	1 2 3 4 5 6 7 8 9
On the bus	Yes	No	1 2 3 4 5 6 7 8 9

·· For Office Use Only ··

Total number of problem settings _____ Mean severity score _____

Note. From *Hyperactive Children: A Handbook for Diagnosis and Treatment* (p. 142) by R. A. Barkley, 1981, New York: Guilford Press. Copyright 1981 by The Guilford Press. Reprinted by permission.

RECORDING OBSERVATIONS OF PARENT-CHILD INTERACTIONS

CODING INSTRUCTIONS

Provide the parent with a list of tasks to do with the child. Some suggestions for tasks are listed in Part 1 of the manual accompanying these handouts. Observe the parent and child for 10 minutes. During this time, record their behavior using the scoring sheet that follows. Instructions for scoring are provided below.

BEHAVIOR CATEGORIES AND DEFINITIONS

The following definitions apply to each of the behavioral categories provided on the coding sheet for recording parent–child interactions.

Original Command (C)

In this category are direct commands or statements that contain imperatives or indirectly stated or implied commands that may be stated as interrogatives. Examples include

- Imperatives
    Come here and . . . .
    Let me . . . .
    Put this . . . .
    I want you to . . . .
    Stop that!
    No! (when used to get the child to stop doing something)
    Now you are to . . . .
- Interrogatives
    Will you hand me . . . ?
    Why don't you . . . ?
    Shall we . . . ?
    Can you . . . ?
    Would you . . . ?

In general, a statement is considered a command if it states or implies that an action is required from the child to start something, stop something, or change to doing something else.

Repeat Command (R)

This is any repetition of a command previously given by the parent where no new command has been given by the parent between the original command and its repetition. If the parent gives a new command, gives a different command, and then goes back to repeat the first command, each of these would be scored as original commands (C), not as a repetition of a command. Examples:

- "Pick up the crayon. . . . Pick it up! I said, pick up that crayon!" (This would be scored as an original command (C), then two repeat commands (R) on the coding sheet.)
- "Pick up the crayon. . . . Get me that block. . . . Now, go back and pick up that crayon like I told you to do." (This would be scored as three original commands (C), since a different command was placed between the first command and its repetition.)

Child Compliance (Cpy)

This category is scored when the child's behavior is in direct response to the parent's command and fulfills the action required by the parent. Any degree of compliance, from approximation to full compliance, is scored in this category. Even if the child is having a tantrum, as long as he or she has begun to comply with what was requested by the parent, the child is scored as having complied with the command. Compliance is scored only if it is initiated within 10 seconds of the original command given by the parent and is scored only once to that original command. Compliance to repeat commands is not scored.

Child Noncompliance (Ncpy)

This category is scored if the child fails to initiate compliance to a parent's command within 10 seconds after the original command was given.

Child Negative (Neg)

This category is scored if the child engages in verbal or nonverbal behavior that conveys refusal, anger, or discouragement in direct response to a parent's original command (C) or a repeat command (R). Examples are saying "No!" to a parent's command, whining, hitting, kicking, saying "I don't want to," pushing, throwing things, pulling away sharply from the parent's grasp, throwing tantrums, crying, swearing or name-calling at the parent, or displaying other negative reactions to the parent's interactions. The category can be scored only once during a command—repeat command sequence. Once the parent shifts to a new original command (C), the category can be scored again.

Parent Approval (A)

This category contains both verbal and nonverbal actions that convey parental approval, encouragement, or acceptance of the child's activities. Clearly, some judgment is required as to the context and emotional tone of these remarks or gestures. In general, when these responses follow the completion of an activity by the child, they are scored as praise. Examples:

- Verbal: OK, Good, That's fine . . . , I like it when you . . . , Terrific!, That was very nice . . . ,
- Nonverbal: Pat on the back, hug, kiss, clapping for child's performance, gestures of approval such as the thumbs-up sign, winking at child.

Parent Negative (PNeg)

This category includes both verbal statements and nonverbal actions conveying discouragement, nonacceptance, or disapproval of the child's activities. Again, some judgment is required concerning the context and emotional tone accompanying the gesture or action. Examples:

- Verbal (direct)
  "No, don't do that . . . !"
  "Stop!"
  "Quit that . . . !"
  "You're a bad boy/girl."

"That's all wrong . . ."
"That's not right . . ."
"I don't like that . . ."
* Verbal (indirect)
  "You're acting like a baby . . ."
  "You'd better watch it or . . ."
  "[Child's name]!!!" (in negative tone)
* Nonverbal
  Spank
  Hit
  Pinch
  Yank at child
  Shove child
  Shaking head "no"
  Raising hand in threatening gesture
  Shaking a finger at child in disapproval

Sometimes, parents may issue a repeat command with a threat, such as "If you don't pick up those toys, I'll spank you!" This would be scored as parent negative (PNeg) rather than as a repeat command (R).

SCORING

1. Number of parent's commands per minute. Count all of the circled Cs on the coding sheet and divide by the number of minutes of coding time.

2. Number of repeat commands per original command. Count all of the Rs circled on the coding sheet and divide by the number of Cs (commands).

3. Child compliance percent. The number of Cpys circled on the coding sheet divided by the number of Cs circled.

4. Percent of child negative per command. The number of Negs circled on the coding sheet divided by the number of Cs.

5. Number of parent approvals per minute. The number of As circled on the coding sheet divided by the number of minutes of observation.

6. Number of parent negatives per minute. The number of PNegs circled on the coding sheet divided by the number of minutes of observation.

CODING

Use a tape recorder with a cassette tape that has been recorded with the verbal cue of "Begin minute 1 . . . Begin minute 2 . . . ," etc., to mark the beginning of each minute. Use the row of the coding sheet corresponding to each minute of observation for recording parent–child interactions in that minute. A coding form contains enough rows for 10 minutes of observation. Since at least 10 minutes of observation are recommended, one form will be used. Each row contains five rectangles and each rectangle corresponds to interactions surrounding each original command issued by the parent. The rectangles are numbered at the top of each column of the coding sheet. This allows space for recording up to five original commands issued by the parent per minute.

When the observations begin, start coding in row 1, the first column (rectangle). Circle a C if the parent gives a command and Cpy if the child begins to comply within 10 seconds of that command or Ncpy if the child fails to begin compliance within 10 seconds. The 10-second interval is determined simply by having the coder count slowly to approximate the time (i.e., one–one thousand, two–one thousand, etc.). A stop watch can be used for more accurate measurement but is not usually necessary. Circle Rs for all repeated commands. Circle As if the parent provides praise or approval to the child during this interaction or PNegs if disapproval is expressed by the parent. As soon as the parent issues a new command, move to the next column (or rectangle) to the right and begin coding all interactions in this block until another new command is given, at which point move to column 3 and begin coding in this block. When the tape recorder announces the beginning of a new minute, move down to row 2 and begin coding again in column 1 (first rectangle in this row). The next command given by the parent, even if it is a repetition of one given in the previous minute, is scored as an original command. Follow this same procedure for each minute of coding.

In general, remember to move across columns to mark the start of each original command and to move down the rows to begin each new minute of coding.

CODING FORM FOR RECORDING PARENT-CHILD INTERACTIONS

min.	Par.	Child	Par.	Par.	Child	Par.
		1			**2**	
1	C R R R R R R R R	Cpy Ncpy Neg	A PNeg	C R R R R R R R R	Cpy Ncpy Neg	A PNeg
2	C R R R R R R R R	Cpy Ncpy Neg	A PNeg	C R R R R R R R R	Cpy Ncpy Neg	A PNeg
3	C R R R R R R R R	Cpy Ncpy Neg	A PNeg	C R R R R R R R R	Cpy Ncpy Neg	A PNeg
4	C R R R R R R R R	Cpy Ncpy Neg	A PNeg	C R R R R R R R R	Cpy Ncpy Neg	A PNeg
5	C R R R R R R R R	Cpy Ncpy Neg	A PNeg	C R R R R R R R R	Cpy Ncpy Neg	A PNeg
6	C R R R R R R R R	Cpy Ncpy Neg	A PNeg	C R R R R R R R R	Cpy Ncpy Neg	A PNeg
7	C R R R R R R R R	Cpy Ncpy Neg	A PNeg	C R R R R R R R R	Cpy Ncpy Neg	A PNeg
8	C R R R R R R R R	Cpy Ncpy Neg	A PNeg	C R R R R R R R R	Cpy Ncpy Neg	A PNeg
9	C R R R R R R R R	Cpy Ncpy Neg	A PNeg	C R R R R R R R R	Cpy Ncpy Neg	A PNeg
10	C R R R R R R R R	Cpy Ncpy Neg	A PNeg	C R R R R R R R R	Cpy Ncpy Neg	A PNeg

Note. From *Hyperactive Children: A Handbook for Diagnosis and Treatment* (p. 162-163) by R. A. Barkley, 1981, New York: Guilford Press. Copyright 1981 by The Guilford Press. Adapted by permission.

	3			4			5	
Par.	Child	Par.	Par.	Child	Par.	Par.	Child	Par.
C R R	Cpy	A	C R R	Cpy	A	C R R	Cpy	A
R R R	Ncpy		R R R	Ncpy		R R R	Ncpy	
R R R	Neg	PNeg	R R R	Neg	PNeg	R R R	Neg	PNeg
C R R	Cpy	A	C R R	Cpy	A	C R R	Cpy	A
R R R	Ncpy		R R R	Ncpy		R R R	Ncpy	
R R R	Neg	PNeg	R R R	Neg	PNeg	R R R	Neg	PNeg
C R R	Cpy	A	C R R	Cpy	A	C R R	Cpy	A
R R R	Ncpy		R R R	Ncpy		R R R	Ncpy	
R R R	Neg	PNeg	R R R	Neg	PNeg	R R R	Neg	PNeg
C R R	Cpy	A	C R R	Cpy	A	C R R	Cpy	A
R R R	Ncpy		R R R	Ncpy		R R R	Ncpy	
R R R	Neg	PNeg	R R R	Neg	PNeg	R R R	Neg	PNeg
C R R	Cpy	A	C R R	Cpy	A	C R R	Cpy	A
R R R	Ncpy		R R R	Ncpy		R R R	Ncpy	
R R R	Neg	PNeg	R R R	Neg	PNeg	R R R	Neg	PNeg
C R R	Cpy	A	C R R	Cpy	A	C R R	Cpy	A
R R R	Ncpy		R R R	Ncpy		R R R	Ncpy	
R R R	Neg	PNeg	R R R	Neg	PNeg	R R R	Neg	PNeg
C R R	Cpy	A	C R R	Cpy	A	C R R	Cpy	A
R R R	Ncpy		R R R	Ncpy		R R R	Ncpy	
R R R	Neg	PNeg	R R R	Neg	PNeg	R R R	Neg	PNeg
C R R	Cpy	A	C R R	Cpy	A	C R R	Cpy	A
R R R	Ncpy		R R R	Ncpy		R R R	Ncpy	
R R R	Neg	PNeg	R R R	Neg	PNeg	R R R	Neg	PNeg
C R R	Cpy	A	C R R	Cpy	A	C R R	Cpy	A
R R R	Ncpy		R R R	Ncpy		R R R	Ncpy	
R R R	Neg	PNeg	R R R	Neg	PNeg	R R R	Neg	PNeg
C R R	Cpy	A	C R R	Cpy	A	C R R	Cpy	A
R R R	Ncpy		R R R	Ncpy		R R R	Ncpy	
R R R	Neg	PNeg	R R R	Neg	PNeg	R R R	Neg	PNeg
C R R	Cpy	A	C R R	Cpy	A	C R R	Cpy	A
R R R	Ncpy		R R R	Ncpy		R R R	Ncpy	
R R R	Neg	PNeg	R R R	Neg	PNeg	R R R	Neg	PNeg

Abbreviations: Par. = parent; C = parent original command; R = parent repeat command; Cpy = compliance within 10 seconds; Ncpy = noncompliance (failure to comply in 10 seconds); Neg = child negative behavior; A = parent approval and praise; PNeg = parent negative behavior.

PARENT HANDOUT FOR STEP 1:
PROFILE OF CHILD AND PARENT CHARACTERISTICS

Child's name _____ Age _____
Name of parent completing this form _____ Date _____

CHILD CHARACTERISTICS

Please list below any characteristics of your child that you believe may be contributing to the child's behavioral difficulties.

Health problems: _____
Physical problems: _____
Developmental delays: _____
Problems with activity level: _____
Problems with attention span: _____
Problems with impulse control: _____
Emotional problems, irritability: _____
Social behavior problems: _____
Problem responses to stimulation: _____
Habit irregularities: _____
Other problems: _____

PARENT CHARACTERISTICS

List below any problems of your own that you believe may contribute to difficulties you have in managing your child or children.

Health problems: _____
Physical problems: _____
Emotional problems: _____
Thinking problems: _____
Problems with
    Attention span? _____ Activity level? _____
    Impulse control? _____ Moodiness? _____
    Eating? _____ Sleeping? _____
Other? _____

PARENT HANDOUT FOR STEP 1:
FAMILY PROBLEMS INVENTORY

Child's name _____ Date _____
Name of parent completing this form _____

Instructions: During the next week, take some time to complete
this questionnaire. You have been shown that one source of trouble that can contribute to child behavior problems is stress within
the family. This questionnaire is designed to help you take inventory of possible stress events that may be occurring within your
family. We think it is important that you take stock of these stressors and begin thinking about how you might begin to resolve
them, if possible.

Listed below are common areas of stress within families. In
the space provided below each, please write down any problems
that you feel you or your family are having in these areas. Next to
each one under the column marked "Proposed solutions," list what
you believe you can begin to do to help reduce these problems, if
that is possible. Please be as honest as you can—your answers will
be kept confidential.

Problem areas   *Proposed solutions*
1. Family health problems:

2. Marital problems:

3. Financial problems:

4. Behavior problems with other children
in family:

5. Occupational/employment problems:

6. Problems with relatives/in-laws:

7. Problems with friends:

8. Other sources of stress:
(religion, conflict over recreational activities for family, drug
or alcohol abuse, etc.)

Thank you for taking time to complete this inventory. Your therapist will review it and may decide to talk with you privately about
some of these stressors. If you would like your therapist to help
you with any of these problems or refer you to others who may be
able to assist you, please indicate that below by checking yes or no
and simply writing the number of the problem area(s) from above.

_____ YES, I would like help with areas (list numbers): _____.
_____ NO, I do not need help with these problem areas.

PARENT HANDOUT FOR STEP 2:
PAYING ATTENTION TO YOUR CHILD'S GOOD PLAY BEHAVIOR

This step of the program involves learning how to pay attention to your child's desirable behavior during playtime. To learn this, it is first necessary to practice the skills of what we call "paying attention." Later, we will show you how to use these new "attending" skills to increase your child's compliance with commands and requests, as well as other positive behavior. Paying attention to your child's play behavior involves the following:

1. If your child is below 9 years of age, select a time each day that is to become your special time with your child. This can be after other children are off to school in the morning if you have a preschool child, or after school or dinner if your child is of school age. You are to set aside 20 minutes each day at this time in order to practice this special playtime with your child. If your child is 9 years or older, you do not have to choose a standard time each day for this special time. Instead, find a time each day as it may arise when your child seems to be enjoying a play activity alone. Then, stop what you are doing and begin to join in the child's play following the instructions below.

2. No other children are to be involved in this special playtime! If you have other children in your family, either have your spouse look after these children while you play with the problem child or choose a time when the other children are not likely to disturb your special time with this child.

3. If you have set up a standard special playtime each day, then when that time comes around simply say to your child, "Its now our special time to play together, what would you like to do?" The child is to choose the play activity, within reason. This should not be watching television. Any other play activity is fine. If you have not set up a standard special playtime, then simply approach your child while he or she is playing alone and ask if you can join in. In either case, you are not to take control of the play or direct it—the child is to choose the play activity.

4. Relax!!! Casually watch what your child is doing for a few minutes and then join in where it seems appropriate. Do not try to do this special playtime when you are upset, very busy, or planning to

leave the house soon for some errand or trip, as your mind will be preoccupied by these matters and the quality of your attention to your child will be quite poor.

5. After watching your child's play, begin to describe out loud what your child is doing. This is done to show your child that you find his or her play interesting. It is done something like the way a sportscaster might describe a baseball or football game over the radio. It should be somewhat exciting and action oriented, not dull and in a single tone of voice. In other words, occasionally narrate your child's play. Young children really enjoy this. With older children, you should still comment about their play but less so than with a young child.

6. ASK NO QUESTIONS AND GIVE NO COMMANDS!!! This is critical. You are to avoid any questioning of the child where possible, as this is often unnecessary and certainly disruptive to your child's play. It is all right to ask a question to clarify how your child is playing if you are uncertain of what he or she is doing. Otherwise, avoid any questions. Also, give no commands or directions and do not try to teach the child anything during this play. This is your child's special time to relax and enjoy your company, not a time to teach or take over the child's play.

7. Occasionally, provide your child with positive statements of praise, approval, or positive feedback about what you like about his or her play. Be accurate and honest, not excessively flattering. For instance, "I like it when we play quietly like this," "I really enjoy our special time together," or "Look at how nicely you have made that . . ." are all positive, appropriate comments. If you need help thinking of these comments, see the other handout from the session for a list of ways to show approval to your child.

8. If your child begins to misbehave, simply turn away and look elsewhere for a few moments. If the misbehavior continues, then tell your child the special playtime is over and leave the room. Tell your child you will play later when he or she can behave nicely. If the child becomes extremely disruptive, destructive, or abusive during play, discipline the child as you might normally do. Your therapist will teach you effective disciplining later in this program.

9. Each parent is to spend 20 minutes with the child in this special playtime. During the first week, try to do this every day or at least five times in a week. After the first week, try to have this special time at least three to four times per week. You should continue this special playtime indefinitely.

THIS PROGRAM IS EASY TO READ, IT IS NOT EASY TO DO!!! Many parents make mistakes during the first few playtimes, usually by giving too many commands and questions or saying too few positive comments to the child. Don't worry about making such mistakes. Just try harder the next time to improve your attending skills toward your child. You may want to spend this kind of special playtime with the other children in your family, once you have improved your attending skills with the problem child.

PARENT HANDOUT FOR STEP 2:
SUGGESTIONS FOR GIVING POSITIVE FEEDBACK
AND APPROVAL TO YOUR CHILD

- Nonverbal signs of approval
    Hug
    Pat on the head or shoulder
    Affectionate rubbing of hair
    Placing arm around the child
    Smiling
    A light kiss
    Giving a thumbs-up sign
    A wink
- Verbal approval
    I like it when you . . . .
    It's nice when you . . . .
    You sure are a big boy/girl for . . . .
    That was terrific the way you . . . .
    Great job!
    Nice going!
    Terrific!
    Super!
    Fantastic!
    My, you sure act grown up when you . . . .
    You know, 6 months ago you couldn't do that as well as you
        can now—you're really growing up fast!
    Beautiful!
    Wow!
    Wait until I tell your mom/dad how nice you . . . .
    What a nice thing to do . . . .
    You did that all by yourself . . . , way to go.
    Just for behaving so well, you and I will . . . .
    I am very proud of you when you . . . .
    I always enjoy it when we . . . like this.

Note:

1. Always be as immediate as possible with your approval.
DON'T WAIT!

2. Always be specific about what it is that you like.

3. Never give a backhanded compliment, such as "It's about
time you cleaned your room. Why couldn't you do that before?!!"

PARENT HANDOUT FOR STEP 3:
PAYING ATTENTION TO YOUR CHILD'S COMPLIANCE

Although you first learned how to pay attention to your child's play during the special playtimes, you can now use these attending skills to provide approval to your child when he or she follows a command or request. When you give a command, it is necessary that you give the child immediate feedback for how well he or she is doing. Don't just walk away, but stay and attend and positively comment on your child's compliance.

1. As soon as you have given a command or request and your child begins to comply, praise the child for complying, as in

"I like it when you do as I ask."
"It's nice when you do as I say."
"Thanks for doing what mom/dad asked."
"Look at how nice [fast, neat, etc.] you are doing that . . . ."
"Good boy/girl for . . . ."

Or use any other statement that specifically says that you appreciate that they are doing what was asked of them. You can also use some of the methods of approval provided in your handouts for Step 2 of this program.

2. Once you have attended to your child's compliance, if you must you can leave for a few moments but be sure to return frequently to continue praising your child's compliance.

3. If you should find that your child has done a job or chore without being specifically told to do so, this is the time to provide especially positive praise to your child. You may even wish to provide your child with a small privilege for having done the job without being told. This will help your child remember and follow household rules and jobs without always being told to do so.

4. You should begin to use positive attention to your child for virtually every command you may give. In addition, this week you should choose two or three commands your child follows inconsistently. You should make a special effort to praise and attend to your child whenever he or she begins to comply with these particular commands.

SETTING UP COMPLIANCE TRAINING PERIODS

It is very important during the next 1 to 2 weeks that you take a few minutes and specifically train compliance in your child. You can do this very easily. Select a time when your child is not very busy and ask him or her to do very brief favors for you, such as "Hand me a Kleenex [spoon, towel, magazine, etc.]," or "Can you reach that _____ for me." We call these *fetch* commands, and they should involve only a very brief and simple effort from your child. Give about five or six of these in a row during these few minutes. As your child follows each one, be sure to provide specific praise for your child's compliance, such as "I like it when you listen to me," or "It is really nice when you do as I ask," or "Thanks for doing what I asked."

Try to have several of these compliance training periods each day. Because the requests are very simple and brief, most children (even behavior problem children) will do them. This provides an excellent opportunity to catch your child being good and to praise his or her compliance.

PARENT HANDOUT FOR STEP 3:
HOW TO GIVE EFFECTIVE COMMANDS

In our work with many behavior problem children, we have noticed that if parents simply change the way they give commands to their children, they can often achieve significant improvements in the child's compliance. When you are about to give a command or instruction to your child, be sure that you do the following:

1. *Make sure you mean it!* That is, never give a command that you do not intend to see followed up to its completion. When you make a request, plan on backing it up with appropriate consequences, either positive or negative, to show that you mean what you have said.

2. *Do not present the command as a question or favor.* State the command simply, directly, and in a businesslike tone of voice.

3. *Do not give too many commands at once.* Most children are able to follow only one or two instructions at a time. For now, try giving only one specific instruction at a time. If a task you want your child to do is complicated, then break it down into smaller steps and give only one step at a time.

4. *Make sure the child is paying attention to you.* Be sure that you have eye contact with the child. If necessary, gently turn the child's face toward yours to insure that he or she is listening and watching when the command is given.

5. *Reduce all distractions before giving the command.* A very common mistake that parents make is to try to give instructions while a television, stereo, or video game is on. Parents cannot expect children to attend to them when something more entertaining is going on in the room. Either turn off these distractions yourself or tell the child to turn them off before giving the command.

6. *Ask the child to repeat the command.* This need not be done with each request, but can be done if you are not sure your child heard or understood the command. Also, for children with a short attention span, having them repeat the command appears to increase the likelihood they will follow it through.

7. *Make up chore cards.* If your child is old enough to have jobs to do about the home, then you may find it useful to make up a chore card for each job. This can simply be a three-by-five file card. Listed on it are the steps involved in correctly doing that chore. Then, when

you want your child to do the chore, simply hand the child the card and state that this is what you want done. Of course, this is only for children who are old enough to read. These cards can greatly reduce the amount of arguing that occurs over whether a child has done a job or chore properly. You might also indicate on the card how much time the chore should take and then set your kitchen timer for this time period so the child knows exactly when it is to be done.

If you follow these seven steps, you will find some improvement in your child's compliance with your requests. When used with the other methods your therapist will teach you, remarkable improvements can occur in how well your child listens and behaves.

PARENT HANDOUT FOR STEP 4:
PAYING ATTENTION WHEN YOUR CHILD
IS NOT BOTHERING YOU

Many parents of behavior problem children complain that they are unable to do things, such as talk on the phone, cook dinner, or visit with a neighbor, without the child interrupting what they are doing. The following steps were designed to help you teach your child to play independently of you when you must be busy with some other activity. It is a very simple procedure that requires you to pay attention and praise your child for staying away and not interrupting you. Many parents provide a lot of attention to a child who is interrupting them but almost no attention to the child when he or she stays away, plays independently, and does not interrupt. No wonder kids interrupt parents so much! To teach your child to stay away from you when you are busy, do the following:

1. When you are about to become occupied with some activity, such as a phone call, reading, or fixing dinner, give your child a direct command. This command should contain two instructions. One part of it tells the child what he or she is to be doing while you are busy, and the second part specifically tells them not to interrupt or bother you. For instance, you can say "Mom has to talk on the telephone, so I want you to stay in this room and watch television and don't bother me." Remember, give the child something to do and say you do not want to be bothered while you are busy.

2. Then as you begin your activity, stop what you are doing after a moment, go to the child, and praise the child for staying away and not interrupting. Remind the child to stay with their assigned task and not to bother you. Return to what you were doing.

3. Then wait a few moments longer before returning to the child and again praising him or her for not bothering you. Return to your activity, wait a little longer, and again praise the child.

4. Over time, what you are trying to do is to gradually reduce how often you praise the child for not bothering you while you increase the length of time you can stay at your own task. Initially, you will have to interrupt what you are doing and go praise the child very frequently, say every 30 seconds to 2 minutes. After a few times like this, wait 3 minutes before praising the child. Then wait 5 minutes before praising the child. Each time, you return to what you are

working on for a slightly longer period of time before going back to praise the child.

5. If it sounds like your child is about to leave what he or she was doing and come to bother you, immediately stop what you are doing, go to the child, praise them for not interrupting you, and redirect them to stay with the task you gave them. The task you give a child should *not* be a chore, but some interesting activity such as coloring, playing with a toy, watching television, or cutting out pictures.

6. By gradually decreasing how often you praise the child, you will be able to stay with your own task for longer and longer time periods while your child does not interrupt you. As soon as you finish what you are doing, go and provide special praise to your child for letting you complete your task. You may even periodically give your child a small privilege or reward for having left you alone while you worked on your project.

Here are some of the activities that parents normally do, during which you should try this method to keep your child from bothering you:

Preparing a meal	Accomplishing any special project
Talking to an adult	Using the telephone
Writing a letter	Reading or watching television
Doing paperwork	Visiting other's homes
Talking at the dinner table	Housecleaning

You should choose one or two of these types of activity with which you will practice this method this week. If you choose talking on the phone, you might want to have your spouse or a friend call you once or twice a day simply as a time to practice this method. That way, when important calls do come in, you have already trained your child to begin to stay away from you so you can handle these calls with less interruption.

PARENT HANDOUT FOR STEP 5:
THE HOME POKER CHIP/POINT SYSTEM

When trying to manage a child with behavioral problems, it is common to find that praise is not enough to motivate the child to do chores, follow rules, or to obey commands. As a result, it is necessary to set up a more powerful program to motivate the child. One such program that has been very successful with children is the home poker chip program (for children 4 to 8 years old) or the home point system (for 9-year-olds and older children). Your therapist will explain in detail how to set up such a program, but here are the steps to follow.

THE HOME POKER CHIP PROGRAM

1. Find or buy a set of plastic poker chips. If the child is 4 or 5 years old, then each chip, regardless of color, represents one chip. For 6- to 8-year-olds, the colors can represent different amounts: white = 1 chip, blue = 5 chips, and red = 10 chips. If you use the colors this way, take one of each color, tape it to a small piece of cardboard, and write on each chip how many chips it is worth. Post this card somewhere so your child can easily refer to it.

2. Sit down and explain to your child that you feel he or she has not been rewarded enough for doing nice things at home and you want to change all that. You want to set up a new reward program so your child can earn privileges and nice things for behaving properly. This sets a very positive tone to the program.

3. You and your child should make a bank in which he or she will keep the chips they will earn. A shoe box, coffee can (with a dull edge on the rim), a plastic jar, etc., can serve as a bank. Have some fun decorating it with your child.

4. Now, you and your child should make up a list of the privileges you want your child to earn with the poker chips. These should include not only occasional special privileges (going to movies, roller-skating, buying a toy) but also the everyday privileges your child takes for granted (television, video games, special toys already in the home, riding a bike, going over to a friend's home, etc.). Your therapist will explain what types of privileges you might include on this list. Be sure to have at least 10, and preferably 15, rewards on this list.

5. Now make up a second list that will contain the jobs and chores you often ask this child to perform. These can be typical household chores such as setting the table for a meal, clearing the table after a meal, cleaning a bedroom, making a bed, and emptying wastebaskets. Also put on the list things like getting dressed for school, getting ready for bed, washing and bathing, brushing teeth, or any other self-help task you give a child that normally poses a problem. Your therapist can help you decide what types of jobs to put on this list for your child's age group and special problems.

6. Next, take each job or chore and decide how much you feel it is worth in chips. For 4- and 5-year-olds, assign from one to three chips for most tasks, and perhaps five for really big jobs. For 6- to 8-year-olds, use a range of 1 to 10 chips and perhaps give a larger amount for big jobs. Remember, the harder the job, the more chips you will pay.

7. Take a moment and add up approximately how many chips you think your child will earn in a typical day if he or she does most of these jobs. Then, remembering this number, decide how many chips your child should have to pay for each of the rewards you listed. We generally suggest that two thirds of the child's daily chips should be spent on typical daily privileges. This allows the child to save about one third of his or her chips every day toward the purchase of some of the very special rewards on the list. Don't worry about the exact numbers to use here. Just use your judgment as to how much each reward should cost, be fair, and charge more chips for the special rewards and less for the daily ones.

8. Be sure to tell your child that he or she will have a chance to earn bonus chips when chores are performed in a prompt and pleasant manner. You will not give these bonus chips all the time but should give them when your child has done a job in an especially pleasant and prompt manner.

9. Be sure to tell the child that chips will only be given for jobs that are done on the first request. If you have to repeat a command, the child will not receive any chips for doing it.

10. Finally, be sure to go out of your way this week to give chips away for any small appropriate behavior. Remember, you can reward a child even for good behaviors that are not on the list of jobs. Be alert for opportunities to reward the child.

Note: DO NOT TAKE CHIPS AWAY THIS WEEK FOR MISBE-HAVIOR!!! You can do that when your therapist tells you to, but otherwise chips are to be used ONLY as rewards this week, not taken away as punishment.

THE HOME POINT SYSTEM

1. Get a notebook, and set it up like a checkbook with five columns, one each for the date, the item, deposits, withdrawals, and the running balance. When your child is rewarded with points, write the job in under "item" and enter the amount as a "deposit." Add it to the child's balance. When your child buys a privilege with his or her points, note the privilege under "item," place this amount in the withdrawal column, and deduct this amount from the "balance." The program works just like the chip system except that you record points in the book instead of giving poker chips.

2. Make up the lists of rewards and privileges and jobs as in the chip program above. Be sure to give the same explanation to the child as to why the point system is being set up. Again, your therapist can help you with these lists.

3. When you get ready to determine how much each job should be paid in points, use larger numbers than in the chip program. We generally use a range of 5 to 25 points for most daily jobs and up to 200 points for very big jobs.

4. Then add up how many points you feel your child will earn on an average day for doing routine jobs. Use this number to decide how much to charge for each privilege. Be sure the child has about one third of his or her daily points free to save up for special privileges. Your therapist can help you in deciding how much to charge for each reward.

5. Follow the same guidelines in using the point system this week. Only parents are to write in the point notebook.

OTHER REMINDERS

Review the list of rewards and jobs every month or so and add new ones to each list as you deem necessary. Check with your child for new rewards he or she may want on the list.

You can reward your child with chips or points for almost any form of good behavior. They can even be used in conjunction with Step 3 to reward your child for not bothering or interrupting your work.

Do not give the chips or points away before the child has done what he or she was told to do, only afterwards. But be as quick as possible in rewarding the child for compliance. Don't wait to reward!

Both parents should use the chip or point system to make it as effective as possible.

When you give points or chips for good behavior, smile, and tell the child what you like that he or she has done.

PARENT HANDOUT FOR STEP 6:
TIME OUT!

This is the most critical part of this program. It requires great skill and care to use this time out method with children when they misbehave or fail to comply with a command. NEVER give a command that you do not intend to back up with consequences if necessary to see that the job gets done. ALWAYS provide praise and approval to your child for obeying the first request made. TRY as much as possible never to repeat a command after it has been said once to the child. To use time out with your child, do the following:

1. Always give your first command to a child in a firm but pleasant voice. DO NOT yell it at the child but also do not ask it as a favor. Follow the suggestions given in Step 3 for giving effective commands. Make it a simple, direct statement to the child in a businesslike tone of voice.

2. After you have given the command, count to five to yourself. Do not count out loud, as the child will eventually come to rely on this counting in learning when to comply with a command.

3. If the child has not made a move to comply within these 5 seconds, you should make direct eye contact, raise your voice to a much louder level, adopt a firm posture or stance, and say,

"If you don't [do what I asked], then you are going to sit in that chair!" (Point to the chair in the corner.)

4. Once you give this warning, count to five again.

5. If the child has not started to comply within these 5 seconds, then take the child firmly by the wrist or upper arm and say,

"You did not do as I asked, so you must go to the chair!"

You should say this loudly and firmly and take the child to the time out chair. The child is to go to the chair immediately, regardless of any promises he or she may make. If the child resists, use slight physical force if need be. The child is not to go to the bathroom, get a drink, or stand and argue with the parent. The child is to be taken immediately to the time out chair.

6. Place the child in the chair, and say sternly,

"You stay there until I tell you to get up!"

You may tell the child that you are not coming back to the chair until he or she has become quiet, but don't say this more than once.

7. Do not argue with the child while he or she is in time out. No one else is to talk to the child during this time. Instead, you should go back to doing your previous work but be sure to keep an eye on what the child is doing in the chair. When the child has served the appropriate time (see below), then return to the child and say,

"Are you ready to do as I asked?"

If the child did something he or she cannot correct, such as swear or hit, then the child is simply to promise not to do that again.

8. At this point, the child is to go do what he or she was told to do before going to time out. The parent should then say in a neutral tone of voice, "I like it when you do as I say."

9. Watch for the next appropriate behavior by your child, and praise the child for it. This insures that the child always receives as much reward as punishment in this program and shows that you are not angry at him or her but at what the child did.

HOW LONG SHOULD THE CHILD STAY IN TIME OUT?

Your child should stay in time out until three conditions are met.

1. The child must always serve a "minimum sentence" when sent to time out. This should be about 1 to 2 minutes for each year of his or her age. Use the 1-minute rule for misbehavior that is mild to moderate, and the 2-minute guideline for serious misbehavior.

2. Once the minimum sentence is over, wait until the child is quiet. Initially, this may take several minutes to an hour or longer the first time your child is sent to time out. You are not to go to the child until he or she has been quiet for a few moments (about 30 seconds or so), even if it means the child remains in time out for up to 1 or 2 hours because he or she is arguing, throwing a tantrum, screaming, or crying loudly.

3. Once the child has been quiet for a few moments, the child must agree to do what he or she was told to do. If it was a chore, the child must agree to do it. If it is something the child cannot correct, such as swearing or lying, the child is to promise not to do it again. If the child fails to agree to do what was asked (says "No!"), instruct

the child to sit in the chair until you give permission to leave. The child is then to serve another minimum sentence, become quiet, and agree to do what was asked. The child is not to leave the chair until he or she has agreed to do the command originally given.

WHAT IF THE CHILD LEAVES THE CHAIR WITHOUT PERMISSION?

Many children will test their parents' authority when time out is first used. They will try to escape from the chair before time is up. Your therapist will discuss with you what actions you should take in punishing your child for leaving the chair. We recommend that the following be done.

1. The first time the child leaves the chair, put him or her back in the chair and say, loudly and with a stern appearance,

> "If you get out of that chair again, I am going to spank you!!" (Clap your hands loudly in front of the child when you say the word "spank.")

2. When the child leaves the chair again, you are to sit in the chair, take the child over your knee, and spank the child using two (and only two!) swift smacks across the buttocks. You need not take the child's pants down to do this. YOU ARE NOT TO HIT THE CHILD WITH ANY OBJECT OTHER THAN YOUR HAND!!! Return the child to the chair and say,

> "Now you stay there until I say you can get up!"

3. Thereafter the child is to be spanked each time that he or she leaves the chair. This is true even if the child is sent to time out again for some other misbehavior. If the child leaves the chair without permission, DO NOT give the warning again, but go straight to the spanking described above.

If you disagree with this method, then your therapist will discuss other alternatives you may use instead of spanking. However, the spanking procedure has been shown to be quite effective, and the vast majority of children require less than two or three spankings total before learning to stay on the chair when told to go there. Many do not even need one spanking, provided the warning described above is given properly.

If the spanking is used, it should only be used for leaving the chair without permission, not for any other form of misbehavior.

Note: If the child requires more than four spankings because he or she continues to leave the chair without permission during a single incident of time out, then do not give any more spankings at that point. Instead, you can use a method of physically restraining the child that your therapist will explain to you.

WHAT SHOULD I CONSIDER AS "LEAVING THE CHAIR?"

Generally, a child is considered to have left the chair if both buttocks leave the flat seat of the chair. Thus, the child can swivel about in the chair and does not have to face the wall, but if his or her buttocks leave the seat of the chair, the procedure described above is to be followed. We also consider rocking the chair and tipping it over as leaving the chair. The child should be warned about this.

WHERE SHOULD THE CHAIR BE PLACED?

The chair should be a straight-backed, dinette-style chair. It should be placed in a corner far enough away from the wall that the child cannot kick the wall while in the chair. There should be no play objects nearby, and the child should not be able to watch television from the chair. Most parents use a corner of a kitchen, first-floor laundry room, the foyer or entry area of a home, the middle or end of a long hallway, or a corner of a living room (not occupied by others). The location should be such that parents can observe the child while continuing about their business. Do not use bathrooms, closets, or the child's bedroom. Sometimes, the child can be told to sit in the middle of a stairway going to a second floor of the home, but a chair is usually preferred.

WHAT TO EXPECT THIS WEEK

If your child follows the pattern typical of most behavior problem children, you can expect that he or she will become quite upset when first sent to time out. Children may become quite angry and vocal while in time out or may cry because their feelings have been hurt. For many children, this prolonged tantrum or crying results in their having to remain in time out well past their minimum sentence because they are not yet quiet. They may therefore spend anywhere from 30 minutes to 1 or 2 hours during the first time out before becoming quiet and agreeing to do what was asked of them. With each use of time out after that, you will find your child becoming quiet much sooner. Eventually, the child will be quiet for most or all of the minimum sentence and will agree to do what was asked immediately thereafter. You will also find that your child will begin to obey your first commands, or at least your warnings about time out, so that the frequency of time out eventually decreases. However, this may take several weeks to achieve. Try to remember during this first week of time out that you are not harming your child, but helping to teach him or her better self-control, respect for parental authority, and the ability to follow rules. Your child may not be happy with this method, but sometimes children must experience unhappiness if they are to learn certain rules expected to be followed within families and society.

REMINDERS

The child is not to leave the time out chair to use the bathroom or get a drink until the time is up and he or she has done what was asked. If children are permitted to do so, they will come to use this demand as a means of escaping from time out on each occasion they are placed in the chair. In addition, if a child is placed in time out during a meal, the child is to miss that meal or that portion of mealtime that was spent sitting in the chair. No effort is made to prepare the child a special snack later to compensate for having missed the meal. What makes time out effective is what your child misses while in the chair, and so efforts should not be made to make up for anything the child misses while in time out. Your therapist will discuss with you many ploys children use to try to escape the chair before their time is up. Be sure to ask how to handle each one of them.

If you expect your child will become physically aggressive with you when you try to use time out, ask your therapist how to deal with this situation.

You are to use the time out method for only one or two types of noncompliance during the next week. This prevents your child from being punished excessively at the start of this program. Your therapist will explain these restrictions to you.

If your child is to be spanked for leaving time out, remember to do so no more than four times during any single incident of time out.

IF YOU HAVE ANY PROBLEMS WITH THIS PROCEDURE, CALL YOUR THERAPIST IMMEDIATELY! Your therapist will provide you with telephone numbers where to reach him or her this week should you have problems with this method.

If you want to use the time out method for bedtime behavior problems, ask your therapist about a slight modification to the procedure for that occasion.

Do not use this procedure out of the home until your therapist tells you to do so.

PARENT HANDOUT FOR STEP 8:
MANAGING CHILDREN IN PUBLIC PLACES

After your child has been trained to comply with commands at home, it will be easier to teach the child to do so in public places, such as stores, restaurants, shopping malls, and church. The key to successfully managing children in public places is to establish a plan that you will follow in dealing with your child and to make sure that your child is aware of this plan BEFORE you go into the public place. There are three easy rules to follow before you enter any public place.

RULE #1: SET UP THE RULES BEFORE ENTERING
THE PLACE

Just before you are about to enter a public place, STOP!!! Stand aside and let others enter the place, but you are not to do so until you have reviewed the important rules of conduct with your child. For instance, for a store the rules for a young child might be "Stand close, don't touch, and don't beg." For an older child, they might be "Stay next to me, don't ask for anything, and do as I say." Give your child about three rules to follow. These should be rules that are commonly violated by the child in that particular place. After you have told the child the rules, the child is to say them back to you. You and your child are not to enter the place until the child has said these rules. If your child refuses to say them, then warn your child he or she will be placed in time out in the car. If the child still refuses, then return to your car and place the child in time out there for failing to comply with your request.

RULE #2: SET UP AN INCENTIVE FOR
THE CHILD'S COMPLIANCE

While still standing in front of the place, tell your child what he or she will earn for adhering to the rules you have just specified and for behaving appropriately in the place. For children who are on a poker chip or point system, these can be used. For children too young for those systems, take along a small bag of snack food (peanuts, raisins, pretzels, corn chips, etc.) to dispense to your child for good behavior throughout the trip. On occasion, you may wish to promise your child a purchase of some sort at the end of the trip, but this should only be done on rare occasions and for exceptionally good behavior during the trip so the child does not come to expect such a purchase as a routine part of any trip away from home. Some parents occasionally promise the child a special privilege at home after the trip. This is fine, but where possible use your chip or point system, as it allows you to reward the child immediately during the trip for good behavior.

RULE #3: SET UP YOUR PUNISHMENT FOR NONCOMPLIANCE

While still outside the place, tell your child what the punishment will be for not following the rules or for misbehavior. In most cases, this will be the loss of points or chips for minor rule violations and the use of time out for moderate to major misbehavior or noncompliance. Do not be afraid to use the time out method in a public place, as it is the most effective method for teaching the child to obey rules in such places. After you have explained the punishment to the child, then you may enter the public place. Upon doing so, you should begin immediately to do two things: Look about the public place for a convenient time out location if you should need one, and attend to and praise your child for following the rules.

If you are using your poker chip or point system, you should give chips or points to your child periodically throughout the trip rather than waiting until the end to provide the reward. In addition, frequent praise and attention should be given to the child for obeying the rules.

If your child starts to misbehave, IMMEDIATELY take away chips or points or place the child in time out. Do not repeat commands or warnings to the child, as the child was forewarned as to what would happen if he or she misbehaved. Here are some convenient time out places:

In Department Stores

Take the child to an aisle that is not used a lot by others and place the child facing a dull side of a display counter or a corner; take the child to the coats section and have him or her face the coat rack; use the gift wrap or credit department area where there is a dull corner; use a dull corner of a restroom; use a changing or dressing room if nearby; use a maternity section (it is not very busy and there are sympathetic moms there).

In Grocery Stores

Have the child face the side of a frozen foods counter (avoid the urge to put the child in the counter itself!); take the child to the furthest corner of the store; find the greeting card display and have the child face the dull side of the counter while you look at cards. Most grocery stores are difficult for finding a time out place, so you may have to use one of the alternatives to time out listed below.

In Church

Take the child to the "crying room" found in most churches, where mothers take irritable babies during the service; use the foyer or entryway to the church; use a restroom off the lobby of the church.

In a Restaurant

Use the restrooms or one of the alternatives listed below.

In Another's Home

Be sure to explain to them that you are using a new child-management method and you may need to place your child in a chair or stand the child in a dull corner somewhere if misbehavior develops. Ask them where one could be used. If this cannot be done in the other's home, then use one of the alternatives listed below.

During a Long Car Trip

Review the rules with the child and set up your incentive before having the child enter the car. Be sure to take along games or activities for the child to do during the trip. If you need to punish the child, pull off the road to a safe stopping area and have the child serve the time out on the floor of the back seat. Never leave the child in the car unattended.

If you use time out in a public place, the minimum sentence needs to be only a half of what it normally is at home, since time out in public places is very effective with children. Also, if the child leaves time out without permission, use the same punishment you have been using at home for this (usually only one swift spank to the buttocks is needed in such cases).

IF YOU CANNOT USE TIME OUT IN THE PUBLIC PLACE

There are always a few places where placing your child in a corner for misbehavior is not possible. Here are some alternatives but they should be used ONLY WHERE YOU CANNOT FIND A TIME OUT AREA:

1. Take the child outside of the building and have him or her face the wall.

2. Take the child back to your car and have the child sit on the floor of the back seat. Stay in the front seat or beside the car.

3. Take along a small spiral notepad. Before entering the public place, tell the child that you will write down any episode of misbehavior and the child will have to go to time out as soon as you get home. You will find it helpful to take a picture of the child when he or she is in time out at home and keep this with your notepad. Show this picture to the child in front of the public place and explain that misbehavior will put the child in time out when you return home.

4. Take along a ballpoint or felt-tip pen. Tell the child in front of the public place that if he or she misbehaves, you will place a hash mark on the back of the child's hand. The child will then serve a minimum sentence in time out at home for each hash mark on the hand.

Important Reminder: Whenever you are out with your child, be sure to ACT QUICKLY to deal with misbehavior, so that it does not escalate into a loud confrontation with the child or a temper tantrum. Also, be sure to give frequent praise and rewards throughout the trip to reinforce your child's good behavior.

PARENT HANDOUT FOR STEP 9:
MANAGING FUTURE BEHAVIOR PROBLEMS

At this point, you have learned a wide variety of methods for rewarding or punishing your child's behavior. It is hoped that you have found these methods to be effective in improving your child's conduct. However, all children occasionally develop behavior problems, and there is no reason to think that your child will not develop new problems as he or she grows up. You have the skills to deal with these problems if you will simply take the time to think about them and set up your own management program. Here are some steps to follow if a new problem develops or an old problem returns.

   1. Take out a notebook and begin recording the behavior problem. Try to be specific about what your child is doing wrong. You should record the rule you asked the child to follow that is now being broken, what exactly he or she is doing wrong, and what you are now doing to manage it.

   2. Keep this record for 1 week or so. Then examine it to see what clues it may give you about how to deal with the problem. Many parents find they have returned to some of their old, ineffective habits of dealing with the child and that this has caused the problem. Here are some common mistakes parents return to doing:

   a. Repeating commands too often.
   b. Using ineffective methods for commands. (See Step 3.)
   c. Providing insufficient attention, praise, or a reward to the child for following the rule correctly. You have stopped your poker chip or points system too early.
   d. Not providing discipline immediately for the rule violation.
   e. Stopping your special playtime with the child.

   If you find yourself slipping back to these old habits, correct them. Go back and review your handouts from this program to make sure you are using the methods properly.

   3. If you need to, set up a special program for managing the problem.

   a. Explain to your child exactly what you expect to be done in the problem situation.
   b. Set up a poker chip or point system to reward the child for following the rules.

   c. Use time out immediately each time the problem behavior occurs.

   d. If your notes indicate that the problem seems to be occurring in one particular place or situation, then follow the steps you were taught to use with your child for public places: (i) anticipate the problem, (ii) review the rules just before the problem develops, (iii) review the incentives for good behavior, and (iv) review the punishment for misbehavior.

   e. Keep recording the behavior problem in your notebook so you can tell when it begins to improve.

4. If these methods fail to work, call your therapist for an appointment and bring along your notes.

References

Achenbach, T. M., & Edelbrock, C. (1983). *Manual for the Child Behavior Checklist and Revised Child Behavior Profile*. Burlington, VT: Thomas Achenbach.

Adesso, V. J., & Lipson, J. W. (1981). Group training of parents as therapists for their children. *Behavior Therapy, 12*, 625-633.

Bard, J. (1980). *Rational-emotive therapy in practice*. Champaign, IL: Research Press.

Barkley, R. A. (1981). *Hyperactive children: A handbook for diagnosis and treatment*. New York: Guilford Press.

Barkley, R. A. (1987). Child behavior rating scales and checklists. In M. Rutter, A. H. Tuma & I. Lann (Eds.), *Assessment and diagnosis in child psychopathology*. New York: Guilford Press.

Barkley, R. A., & Edelbrock, C. S. (1987). Assessing situational variation in child behavior problems: The Home and School Situations Questionnaires. In R. Prinz (Ed.), *Advances in behavioral assessment of children and families* (Vol. 3, pp. 157-176). Greenwich, CT: JAI.

Barkley, R., Karlsson, J., Strzelecki, E., & Murphy, J. (1984). Effects of age and Ritalin dosage on the mother-child interactions of hyperactive children. *Journal of Consulting and Clinical Psychology, 52*, 750-758.

Beck, A. T. (1967). *Depression: Causes and treatment*. Philadelphia: University of Pennsylvania Press.

Cairns, R. (1979). *The analysis of social interactions*. New York: LEA.

Christensen, A., Johnson, S. M., Phillips, S., & Glasgow, R. E. (1980). Cost effectiveness of behavioral family therapy. *Behavior Therapy, 11*, 208-226.

Christophersen, E. R., Barnard, S. R., & Barnard, J. D. (1981). The family training program manual: The home chip system. In R. Barkley, *Hyperactive children: A handbook for diagnosis and treatment* (pp. 437-448). New York: Guilford Press.

Dangel, R. F., & Polster, R. A. (1984). *Parent training*. New York: Guilford Press.

Dumas, J. E., & Wahler, R. G. (1983). Predictors of treatment outcome in parent training: Mother insularity and socioeconomic disadvantage. *Behavioral Assessment, 5,* 301-313.

Dyer, W. (1977). *Your erroneous zones.* New York: Avon.

Ellis, A., & Harper, R. (1975). *A new guide to rational living.* New York: Wilshire Book Co.

Eyberg, S. M., & Matarazzo R. G. (1980). Training parents as therapists: A comparison between individual parent-child interaction training and parent group didactic training. *Journal of Clinical Psychology, 36,* 492-499.

Firestone, P., Kelly, M., & Fike, S. (1980). Are fathers necessary in parent training groups? *Journal of Clinical Child Psychology, 9,* 44-47.

Firestone, P., & Witt, J. E. (1982). Characteristics of families completing and prematurely discontinuing a behavioral parent-training program. *Journal of Pediatric Psychology, 7,* 209-222.

Forehand, R., & McMahon, R. (1981). *Helping the noncompliant child: A clinician's guide to parent training.* New York: Guilford Press.

Goyette, C. H., Conners, C. K., & Ulrich, R. F. (1978). Normative data on Revised Conners Parent and Teacher Rating Scales. *Journal of Abnormal Child Psychology, 6,* 221-236.

Johnson, S. M., Wahl, G., Martin, S., & Johansson, S. (1973). How deviant is the normal child? A behavioral analysis of the preschool child and his family. In R. D. Rubin, J. P. Brady, & J. D. Henderson (Eds.), *Advances in behavior therapy* (Vol. 4). New York: Academic Press.

Locke, H., & Wallace, K. (1959). Short marital-adjustment and prediction tests: Their reliability and validity. *Marriage and Family Living, 21,* 251-255.

Martin, B. (1977). Brief family intervention: Effectiveness and the importance of including the father. *Journal of Consulting and Clinical Psychology, 45,* 1002-1010.

Mash, E. J., Hamerlynck, L. A., & Handy, L. C. (1976). *Behavior modification and families.* New York: Brunner/Mazel.

Mash, E. J., Handy, L. C., & Hamerlynck, L. (1976). *Behavior modification approaches to parenting.* New York: Brunner/Mazel.

Mash, E. J., & Terdal, L. (1981). *Behavioral assessment of childhood disorders.* New York: Guilford Press.

Mash, E. J., & Terdal, L. G. (Eds.) (1987). *Behavioral assessment of childhood disorders* (2nd ed.). New York: Guilford Press.

Mash, E. J., Terdal, L., & Anderson, K. (1973). The Response Class Matrix: A procedure for recording parent-child interactions. *Journal of Consulting and Clinical Psychology, 40,* 163-164.

Paternite, C., & Loney, J. (1980). Childhood hyperkinesis: Relationships between symptomatology and home environment. In C. K. Whalen & B. Henker (Eds.), *Hyperactive children: The social ecology of identification and treatment* (pp. 105-144). New York: Academic Press.

Patterson, G. R. (1976). The aggressive child: Victim and architect of a coercive system. In E. J. Mash, L. A. Hamerlynck, & L. C. Handy (Eds.), *Behavior modification and families* (pp. 267-316). New York: Brunner/Mazel.

Patterson, G. R. (1982). *Coercive family process.* Eugene, OR: Castalia.

Pollard, S., Ward, E., & Barkley, R. (1983). The effects of parent training and Ritalin on the parent-child interactions of hyperactive boys. *Child and Family Behavior Therapy, 5,* 51-69.

Prinz, R. (Ed.) (1986) *Advances in behavioral assessment of children and families.* Greenwich, CT: JAI Press.

Robin, A. L. (1979). Problem-solving communication training: A behavioral approach to the treatment of parent-adolescent conflict. *American Journal of Family Therapy, 7,* 69-82.

Robin, A. L. (1981). A controlled evaluation of problem-solving communication training with parent-adolescent conflict. *Behavior Therapy, 12,* 593-609.

Robin, A. L. (1984). Parent-adolescent conflict: A developmental problem of families. In R. McMahon & R. Peters (Eds.), *Childhood disorders: Developmental-behavioral approaches* (pp. 244-266). New York: Brunner/Mazel.

Robin, A. L., & Foster, S. (in press). *Parent-adolescent conflict.* New York: Guilford Press.

Strain, P. S., Young, C. C., & Horowitz, J. (1981). Generalized behavior change and family demographic variables. *Behavior Modification, 5,* 15-26.

Wahler, R. (1975). Some structural aspects of deviant child behavior. *Journal of Applied Behavior Analysis, 8,* 27-42.

Webster-Stratton, C. (1984). Randomized trial of two parent-training programs for families with conduct disordered children. *Journal of Consulting and Clinical Psychology, 52,* 666-678.

Wells, K., & Forehand, R. (1985). Conduct disorders. In P. Bornstein & A. Kazdin (Eds.) *Handbook of behavior therapy with children.* Homewood, IL: Dorsey Press.

Worland, J., Carney, R., Milich, R., & Grame, C. (1980). Does in-home training add to the effectiveness of operant group parent training? *Child Behavior Therapy, 2,* 11-24.

Index